D1094182

Home Winemaker's Handbook

Harper & Row, Publishers • New York, Evanston, and London

Walter S. Taylor and
Richard P. Vine

Home Winemaker's
Handbook

Library of Congress Catalog Card Number: 67-28835
Designed by The Etheredges

To Greyton H. Taylor,
without whose cooperation
over the years this book would not
have been possible

Contents

Preface

The growth of home winemaking in our country is amazing. Our creation of The Winemaker's Shop is a result of this growth. Actually, winemaking is one of the few hobbies we can think of that is so rewarding in so many ways. Besides being a worthwhile pastime, a true expression of the winemaker's art and talent, a topic of endless learning, and inexpensive, it is just plain lots of fun.

We hope this book will fill the need of correct information for the home winemaker and grape grower. It is based on the questions of the thousands of visitors to The Winemaker's Shop and the Finger Lakes Wine Museum. The museum is only a few hundred feet from the shop and was the first independent wine museum in America. The large historical collection of early wine-making and vineyard equipment is unique and is a "must" stopping place for all winemakers and wine lovers.

Sometimes when you start a project such as a book—or a museum—you never realize the scope of the project. For instance, when the Finger Lakes Wine Museum was started, we never considered what was truly behind the great winemaking industry of the Finger Lakes. There were many, many people involved: the grape growers and their families from father to son; the more than 50 wineries of the area, which came and most of which went because of the onslaught of prohibition; the salesmen who sold their wares throughout the United States and all over the world; and the employees of the wineries. Without all of these people working together and having faith in the greatness of our region, we would not be where we are today. Most assuredly, a lot of these enterprises were strictly economical, but many were started because of the love of grape growing and winemaking.

One of the main functions of the museum is to be of help in educating and stimulating people to become interested in wine-making and grape growing. We hope that this book will be a valuable tool for these people, too.

Since there were a number of people involved in the Finger Lakes' winemaking industry, many people helped in the preparing of the book. We wish to thank the following for their aid in the writing of the book: Greyton H. Taylor, Theodore E. Carl, Dr. Richard Wellington, Willam S. Shill, Robert Scharff, Janet Baroody, Thomas Hereford, W. Jeff Heath, Lura Tracy, Judy Oplinger, Philip M. Wagner, Jack McConnell, John P. Tomkins, Shirley Hill, Earl Johnston, W. Michael Konnerth, Janet McCandless, Douglas Moorhead, Dr. Elias J. Amdur, and the editors of *Wines & Vines Magazine*. We also would like to thank our wives, Ellen Taylor and Gaye Vine, for their diligence during our work on this book.

WALTER S. TAYLOR
RICHARD P. VINE

Home Winemaker's Handbook

Chapter One

The Magic of Wine

Most of the world's wine is made at home, not in the commercial winery. While the American head of a family still trails his foreign brother in output, home winemaking in the United States is on an amazing increase. Businessmen, doctors, and lawyers are discovering in their home wineries a quiet retreat from the hectic cares of the day. Engineers, teachers, scientists, craftsmen are finding in the unending mystery of wine's magic a challenge to their skill and knowledge. Country folk, golden agers are discovering in winemaking a pleasant activity that shortens the long hours of fall and winter. Winemaking, in short, offers something to everyone. It is one of the few hobbies that is rewarding in so many ways. Besides being a worthwhile pastime, a true expression of the winemaker's art and talent, a topic of endless learning, and inexpensive, it is just plain lots of fun!

THE STORY OF WINEMAKING

Winemaking, of course, is as old as civilization. So lost in antiquity are the first cultivated vineyards that there is no specific record of the beginning of wine. Geologists have found evidence that grapes were a food of prehistoric man. Since the juice of pressed grapes turns naturally into wine, it is assumed that men drank this beverage before the dawn of history. References to wine are found in the hieroglyphics of ancient Egypt and Babylonia. Wine was made in China before the year 2000 B.C. The Bible tells of the cultivation of the vine in Palestine; archeologists recently unearthed the ruins of a huge, 2,600-year-old winery there, at Gibeon. The writings of the Greeks, Romans, and all historians of ancient times are replete with references to wine as an adjunct to life, health, and happiness.

Wine is mentioned 165 times in the Bible. For instance, the ninth chapter of Genesis has to do with Noah planting a vineyard on Mount Ararat, where his ark came to rest. Subsequently, we learn he made his grapes into wine and drank it. The Pharaohs of Egypt made wine fifty centuries ago. The beauteous Queen Nefertiti used wine as a base for her perfume. The Pharaohs were buried in their Pyramids with grape seeds, that they might not lack wine in the hereafter.

About 600 B.C., the Phoenicians took the "vine that bears wine" to Ancient Greece. Pliny described ninety-one kinds of wine grapes in Greece. (Today, there are some eight thousand named grapes; few of them, however, are wine grapes.) Plato and Socrates and Aristotle and Aeschylus loved and were inspired by wine, and Sappho sang songs of it. You can still buy the self-same wine, *retsina*, infused with resin, that Plato so highly praised and the oracles of Delphi sipped.

The Greeks were the first Europeans to grow wine, and it was they who taught the Romans. Rome, in turn, established wine-growing as an important agricultural pursuit in Western Europe after Caesar's conquest of Gaul. Since the Roman era every country in Europe and along the Mediterranean climatically suited to vine culture has made wine.

Between A.D. 500 and 1400 Europe became the winegrowing center of the world. Minstrels sang of wine and poets penned verses in its praise. It became the universal mealtime beverage, partly, no doubt, because of the unhealthful character of water supplies. To this day wine, along with bread and meat, is one of the staples of life in the principal European wine-consuming countries. So important was wine in these countries in the Middle Ages that few contracts were made without a certain amount of the beverage changing hands. Taxes were collected partly in wine, and bills settled in the same manner.

As the centuries passed, the "magic" of the fermentation of grapes continued. Large wineries arrived through the efforts of the monasteries. Wine was graced with being not only an important food but a very real relief from pain during times when hunger and agony were common. Also wines from different parts of Europe began to take on distinct characteristics disclosing their origin. Spanish winemakers excelled in producing a wine with nutlike flavor called "Jerez" or "sherry." The Portuguese made a very dark sweet red wine called "port" and the vineyards of Bordeaux and Burgundy became famous for their delicious red dinner wines.

The earliest wines of history were, of course, red, made simply by crushing the grapes and fermenting the juice with the pulp and skins of the fruit. White wines, made by drawing off the juice to be fermented alone, came later. To a Benedictine monk, Dom Pérignon, for many years cellarer at the Abbey of Haut-villers, France, has been attributed the discovery in 1679 that, when wine is bottled while a fermentation is in progress, it will bubble and sparkle. Whether or not Dom Pérignon was the actual discoverer of champagne, it is certain that his skillful blending and expert handling of the wine did much to increase its fame.

It was only twenty-six years after the first voyage of Columbus that Cortez, the Spanish conqueror of Mexico, ordered that wine-growing become an industry in the the New World. In issuing several ordinances to further agriculture, Cortez stipulated that certain holders of land grants must plant, each year for five years, one thousand vines for each one hundred Indians living on the land. The vines were European, brought from Spain. Winegrowing increased so rapidly in the New World that Spain, fearing interference with its own wine monopoly, at one time ordered winegrowing stopped and declared all wine not imported from Spain to be contraband.

Winegrowing spread from Mexico northward into California. The Jesuit fathers carried Spanish colonization up the western coast into the Mexican peninsula of Lower California, and their successors, the Franciscans, advanced into what now is the state of California. As each new settlement or mission was established, vines were planted as one of the first steps in transforming a savage wilderness into a state of civilization.

It was the Franciscans and their leader, Padre Junípero Serra, who upon establishing Mission San Diego in 1769 and planting wine grapes there, discovered that California was a land especially favored for winegrowing. Even earlier, while western winegrowing still was confined to Mexico, the English colonists along the eastern seaboard of America were attempting to make wine. The earliest settlers of those colonies wrote enthusiastically about the profusion of wild grapes there, but efforts to make palatable wine from them failed. They then imported European cuttings.

Attempts to cultivate the European vines in eastern regions continued for more than two hundred years, but all failed. The European varieties could not acclimate to the rigors of soil and climate.

In the late 1700's John Dufour, thinking that he had at last succeeded in cultivating a European vine in Kentucky, accidentally began the domestication of wild native vines and gave the first impetus to the development of American grape varieties. In the years that followed many native American grapes were crossbred and domesticated for winemaking. Important among them were the Delaware, Catawba, Concord, Norton, Ives, Niagara, and Scuppernong. The wines of all these grapes are distinctly different from those of European grapes, with spicy flavors and aromas entirely their own. Utilizing these grapes, a large and important wine industry developed in the eastern and middle western states. For example, the Longworth vineyards, near Cincinnati, were famous. Missouri, in pre-Civil War days, thanks largely to German immigration, led the nation in wine production. As far back as

1829 the Reverend William Bostwick, first rector of the newly founded St. James Episcopal Church, in Hammondsport, New York, on Keuka Lake, planted grapevines in his parish yard, whose flourishing growth encouraged others to do likewise. Thus was started the Finger Lakes wine industry, which has today made New York State the leading premium-quality wine and champagne producer from native American grapes as well as the new French and German varieties.

It was not for some thirty years after the Reverend Bostwick's pioneering, however, that champagne production was seriously undertaken in the Finger Lakes district, which has since become famous for that sparkling wine. In 1860, a "sparkling wine factory" was founded on the shores of Keuka Lake by the Pleasant Valley Wine Company. The wine produced was hailed in Boston at the Parker House as the "great Champagne of the Western World," from which was soon born the name "Great Western," which the brand bears today.

Many commercial wineries, large and small, led by such families as Champlin, Putnam, Taylor, and Widmer, soon followed, until at the onset of national prohibition there were some fifty operating in the Keuka-Canandaigua lakes region. The thirteen years of national drought found only a few survivors able to resume winemaking. Today there are but five large wineries operating in the Finger Lakes region, all of them dating from well before the turn of the century. But, thanks to its excellent grape-growing characteristics, the region has made New York the second-largest wine-producing state in the Union.

In California, the largest wine producer in the United States, the Franciscan fathers were the only winegrowers until 1824, and they had not attempted production on a commercial scale. Their wines were grown for religious services, for table use, for treating the sick, and for hospitable entertainment of the travelers who visited the missions. Some of their wines, and also their brandies, were sold in small lots, and their fame began to spread.

Then came the first commercial growers. About 1824 one of the first Americans to settle in California was Joseph Chapman. He set out four thousand vines at the Pueblo of Los Angeles. In 1831 he was followed by Jean Louis Vignes, a Frenchman from the Bordeaux wine district. A few years later the missions had begun to deteriorate and their winegrowing activities were suffering accordingly. Commercial winegrowers were coming into their own and another development of even greater significance had begun. A vital change in the grape varieties used for California wine was taking place.

Vignes was apparently the first to realize that, to produce finer wines, grape varieties choicer than the Spanish or Mission grapes must be brought from Europe. In the early 1830's he sent to France for cuttings of choice grapevines. Chosen and packed with the utmost care, the cuttings were shipped to Boston and then around Cape Horn to California. Vignes reported the cuttings were received in good condition and, upon planting, flourished in his vineyard.

While Vignes started the change from the Mission grape to European varieties, Agoston Haraszthy, a Hungarian nobleman, is credited with being "the father of the commercial wine industry in California." In 1861, he purchased more than 100,000 vine cuttings of about 300 European varieties, and the following year planted many of them in his vineyard at Sonoma. The bulk of the cuttings, however, were sold to growers in all sections of the state. The success of these grape varieties was phenomenal and winegrowing spread into the Napa Valley, the Sierra Nevada foothills, the Livermore Valley, Santa Clara Valley, San Joaquin Valley, Sacramento Valley, the Santa Cruz Mountains, and other sections of the state. The European winemakers attracted by the Gold Rush contributed their centuries-old art to this new California industry, and soon the state reached the stage of being the number one producer of wines in the Western Hemisphere.

While the major wineries are located in California, New York, Ohio, and a few other areas, home winemaking is done in all fifty states and Canada. The amateur uses the same raw material—grapes—and procedures similar to the commercial vintner's. And if he has the know-how and exercises this knowledge skillfully, he can turn out a wine as fine as any produced anywhere on the face of the earth.

WHAT IS WINE?

The question is as old as the beverage. One scientist says wine is the most healthful and hygienic of all beverages. A scientist with a touch of poet in his soul calls it a chemical symphony. A poet says wine is the drink of the gods.

The answer, such as it is to date, takes up several hundred running feet of library shelf, and it keeps getting longer every day. But the answer always goes back to the fundamentals. Wine is the product of normal alcoholic fermentation of the juice of sound, ripe grapes.

Nature has been making wine since the first grape was crushed before the dawn of history. When crushed with its own natural yeast the grape makes out of its own sugar its own alcohol to preserve itself for man's pleasure. The role of the winemaker is to assist and guide nature's "magic."

The refinements of winegrowing are in the choice, planting, cultivating, and harvesting of the grapes; the control of fermentation; care, watchfulness, and sanitation in the winery; proper aging, and expert blending. These are the responsibilities of the men who have selected winemaking as their profession or hobby.

TYPES OF WINES

Wines may be roughly classified into five distinct kinds, namely: red dinner wines, white dinner wines, dessert wines, apéritif wines, and the ever-glamorous sparkling wines. The names describe the wines.

Red Dinner Wines. These are usually dry, suited to accompany main-course dishes. Most red dinner wines are completely dry, and with their rich, sometimes tart and even astringent flavors, blend admirably with red meats, spaghetti, and highly-seasoned foods. The various dry red dinner wine types vary in tartness, body, and flavor. Alcoholic content of red dinner wines is from 10 to 14 percent.

White Dinner Wines. These vary from dry and tart to sweet and full-bodied, with the delicate flavor that blends best with white meats, fowl, and seafoods. They range from pale straw to deep gold in color, and in alcoholic content from 10 to 14 percent.

Dessert Wines. These wines are sweet and full-bodied and are generally served with desserts. They range from medium sweet to sweet and from pale gold to red. The two distinct popular types are *port* and *sherry.* Their alcoholic content is usually about 19 or 20 percent. Grape brandy, which usually has a proof between 175 and 195 degrees, is added to raise the alcohol content from 12 to 20 percent. In commercial production, no other kind of spirits may be added by federal laws and regulations. In fact, the addition of the brandy can be performed only under the supervision of a United States government gauger.

Apéritif Wines. This term usually refers to *vermouth* and other wines of the appetizer class, which are especially flavored with herbs and other aromatic substances. There are two principal vermouth types—dry (French type) and sweet (Italian type). The dry is very pale amber; the sweet, dark amber. Along with the traditional dry vermouth, there has been developed, in recent years, a type called "light dry vermouth." This has the general characteristics of dry vermouth but is extremely pale—almost colorless. In producing vermouth, neutral white wines first are selected and aged. Then they are flavored, either by steeping the herbs in the wine or by adding an infusion of herbs. Further aging follows. Each vermouth producer has his own private, carefully guarded herb formula, some using as many as fifty different herbs, barks, flowers, leaves, and seeds. Vermouth ranges from 15 to 20 percent in alcoholic content.

Sparkling Wines. These are dry dinner wines (enjoyed also with appetizers or desserts, or without food) which have been made naturally effervescent by a second fermentation in closed containers. They are red, pink, or white, and have a wide flavor range. Their alcoholic content usually extends from 10 to 14 percent by volume, as does that of still dinner wines. The most popular types are *champagne* and *sparkling Burgundy.*

Wine Type Names. The wine type names have two main origins. Many of them, like Burgundy, Rhine wine, Sauterne, and the others just mentioned, came into use centuries ago as the names of the wines of Old World viticultural districts famed for those particular types. As the wine types became known throughout the world, the same names were applied to all wines having similar characteristics, wherever grown. Usage established the practice. These are referred to as *generic wine* names and usually have a geographic significance.

Besides generic wines, there are *varietal wines,* a term applied when the type is named from the principal grape used in making it. To bear a varietal name a wine must derive at least 51 percent of its volume from the grape for which it is named, and must have the flavor and aroma of that grape. Some varietal wines are made 100 percent from the grape for which they are named. Others are made from blends of various grapes, once the required 51 percent or more of the wine's volume is assured from the grape whose name appears on the label. Popular varietal wine names include *Delaware, Dutchess, Diamond, Cabernet Sauvignon, Pink Catawba, Isabella Rosé* and *Gamay Beaujolais.*

THE PRINCIPLES OF WINEMAKING

As previously stated, the principles of winemaking, whether on an amateur or professional scale, are the same. The actual techniques, of course, will vary and this is true even among commercial wineries. While only a few hundred yards apart, for instance, several of the winemaking operations of our neighboring winery and the Pleasant Valley Wine Company are *radically* different. However, to set the stage for several of the following chapters, let us take a quick look at how a typical commercial winery operates.

Fig. 1

At the approach of the harvesting season, winery representatives pay repeated visits to the vineyards in the area to meet with viticulturists and make field tests of the grapes to ascertain the degree of ripeness and estimate the tonnage of grapes to be expected from each grower. As full maturity develops in the various varieties of grapes, field representatives gather samples and bring them to the laboratory of the winery, where a complete check is made to supplement the field tests. When it is determined that the grapes are ready for harvesting, a picking and delivery schedule is set up with the grower so that the grapes arrive at the winery as soon as possible after picking, and quantities to arrive on any particular day are governed by a schedule of loads, of no greater amount than can be processed on the day of arrival.

At harvest time, the grapes are picked and put into specially designed picking boxes for transportation to the wineries. As the loads of grapes arrive at the winery, usually at fifteen-minute intervals, they are inspected and weighed. After being weighed they are fed into a stemmer and crusher. Here the stems are removed and the grapes are crushed to a semiliquid consistency, in which condition they are pumped into a stainless steel tank placed directly over the press and equipped with a telescopic outlet for loading the press.

Here we should mention that there are several methods of preparing the grapes for the fermentation tanks and casks:

1. Cold pressing of the crushed grapes as they come from the stemmer and crusher. This is the method generally followed for white wines.

2. Hot pressing for those grapes which are to be used in making red wines. In this method, the crushed grapes are heated in the kettle over the press to 140° to 170° F. prior to loading the press. This is one method for the extraction of the red color of dark grapes.

3. Another method for making red wines is to deposit the crushed grapes in the fermenter, allowing the juice to ferment in direct contact with the skins and pulp of the grapes. After fermentation the juice is drawn off or pressed from the solids. Pink or rosé wines are made by allowing the juice to ferment with the grapes for a short time and then drawing off the juice to finish fermentation alone. There are divergent opinions among profes-

sional vintners as to which method of extracting the color from red grapes is preferred. At our winery we prefer to ferment on the skins.

There are three general methods of pressing the crushed grapes:

1. In a hydraulic press the grapes, either hot or cold, as the case may be, are fed to the press forms from holding tanks as previously explained. The buildup of the press forms consist of a series of press racks between which the grapes are deposited on press cloths, which are usually made of cotton or nylon. The press cloth is placed on a rack, and after the grapes are deposited on the cloth, the ends are folded over and another rack is set on top of this arrangement. The crushed grapes in the press cloths are referred to as "cheeses." A series of fifteen to eighteen, and sometimes twenty-five, such cheeses make up a press and such a setup is then moved over the hydraulic press, where pressure is exerted on the grapes. Actually, the amount of grapes in a fully loaded press

Fig. 2

will vary, depending upon the size of the press. Some presses can handle up to five tons of grapes in one buildup. The press racks are usually about five feet square and the cloths somewhat larger, to enable the crushed grapes to be entirely closed in the cloths between the racks. A small amount of a special cellulose material is added to the crushed grapes to keep the cheeses from skidding sideways in the press and to make it easier to strip the cloths from the pressed cheese (now designated as "pomace") after pressing.

2. An innovation in pressing developed in Western Germany is the Wilmes press. This is a cylindrical-shaped press, equipped with a heavy rubber bag. The crushed grapes are run into the press from the holding tank; much of the juice is run off by whirling the cylinder. After this is done, the press is again filled and drained until the cylinder is filled with the crushed grapes. The cylinder is then closed and the rubber bag is inflated by compressed air, which presses out the remaining juice through holes in the cylinder.

3. Another type of press in common use, known as the Vaslin press, is also cylindrical in shape and is so arranged that the two end plates work toward each other like opposed pistons and express the juice. This press is often called a "horizontal basket press."

Each ton of grapes pressed will yield approximately 175 to 200 gallons of juice. This figure will vary somewhat for the different varieties of grapes and is also dependent upon climatic and other growing conditions prevailing throughout the growing season.

As the fresh grape juice runs from the press, or the wine when it is produced by fermenting on the skins, it is pumped through stainless-steel or Pyrex-glass pipes into the fermentation tanks. Uniform samples of each lot of juice are taken from the fermenters and tested for total solids (mostly grape sugar) and acidity, and when necessary sugar in the form of dextrose or sucrose is added to bring the sugar content of the juice to a level sufficient to produce the desired alcohol percentage during fermentation. For champagne cuvée, or stock, a wine of 11 percent alcohol by volume is desired; for dry table wines, one of between 12 and 12½ percent is wanted; and for wines which are to become dessert wines at a later date, a percentage as close to 13 percent as possible is the goal.

To the fresh juice, or "must" as a winemaker calls it, about 40 to 60 parts per million of sulfur dioxide is added to inhibit the action of the undesirable natural wild yeasts and other micro-organisms naturally present in the grapes. Then the juice is inoculated with a pure-culture wine yeast previously propagated under highly sterile conditions to create the desired fermentation.

Fermentation, as mentioned previously, is the basis of formation of all types of wine. The grape juice, or must, provides the sugar and other substances needed for yeast growth, and the yeast supplies the enzymes by which the sugar of the juice is converted into ethyl alcohol and carbon dioxide gas. Fermentations are conducted at temperatures of 50° to 80° F. Should fermentation temperatures rise above 85°, it becomes necessary to cool the fermenting juice to prevent the danger of a "stuck" fermentation (a condition in which fermentation stops at high temperatures). Such a condition is very dangerous as it would make possible the growth of undesirable organisms which might spoil the wine. Conversely, if temperatures during fermentation drop much below 50°, sometimes it becomes necessary to warm the fermenting juice in order that the process will go to completion.

In the case of juices fermenting on the skins, the pulp, skins, and some of the seeds are brought to the surface by the buoyant effect of the carbon dioxide gas being generated within the tank and specific gravity being lessened by the formation of ethyl alcohol. This forms a massive layer or cap, often two feet or more in thickness. This cap may become so dense that the temperature within it will be several degrees higher than the temperature of the must beneath the cap. Under such conditions there is a distinct danger of spoilage organisms growing in this cap and contaminating the rest of the fermenting mass. For this reason, it is usually the practice to drain some juice from the bottom of the fermenter. This juice is pumped into the top of the fermenter to keep the cap moist. Some fermenters are designed to keep the cap submerged.

In the initial stages, fermentation can be quite violent in action, with considerable foaming; thus it is winery practice to limit quantities of fermenting must to about 70 percent of the capacity of the container. As the alcohol builds up in the fermenting juice, the action subsides to a more moderate rate and the fermenters can be filled almost to capacity, while fermentation continues until all the fermentable sugars have been converted to alcohol and carbon dioxide. After fermentation is completed, as determined by laboratory examination, the fermenters are filled to capacity so that no air space remains in the top of the cask, thus preventing possibility of many types of spoilage and oxidation.

As fermentation progresses, a considerable quantity of yeast is grown, and the tartrates in the form of cream of tartar from the grape juice begin to crystallize out of the solution. This separation of the tartrates takes place because tartar is less soluble in alcohol than it is in water or grape juice, so that, as the percentage of alcohol increases during fermentation, more and more tartrates are precipitated out. Incidentally, newly fermented wine is cloudy and has a pronounced "yeasty" aroma. Upon standing, the yeast gradually settles down to the bottom of the cask. Suspended particles of skin and pulp and the tartrates also settle to the bottom. All this forms a sediment known as "lees."

When laboratory tests confirm that fermentation is complete, the new wine is racked (winery term meaning "decanted") from the lees to aid in clearing and to avoid having the wine pick up possible undesirable flavors and odors from the material in the wine lees. Prompt removal of the yeast cells also improves the keeping qualities of the wine by preventing absorption of constituents present in the yeast. Some wineries filter the new wine, rather than merely racking it from the lees, in order to obtain a better separation of wine from sediment.

The cleared wine is stored in completely filled tanks and care is taken to examine these casks once or twice a week to see that they are kept full. When the wines have been racked and not filtered, the racking process is repeated periodically to aid in the clarification of the new wine. During filtering and racking, the wine loses the carbon dioxide which dissolved in it during fermentation. Care should be taken to prevent oxidation during racking and filtering since this can result in darkening in color and loss of flavor, especially in white wines. It is also important that all wine-moving equipment such as hoses, pumps, and pipe lines be made of special-grade rubber, glass, or stainless steel. Copper, brass, or iron can, even in relatively minute amounts, cause a metal "casse," or cloudiness in the wine, which no amount of filtration will satisfactorily remove.

The rate at which wines reach the proper level of aging varies

Fig. 3

with the kind of wine, the extent of aeration, the type and size of storage container, and the storage temperature. Use of small casks and frequent racking will increase the speed of aging. Temperature markedly affects aging. The lower the temperature, the more speedily the yeasts and other microorganisms become inactive and settle out, and the more rapidly and completely excess cream of tartar, or "wine stone," is precipitated. A wine should, therefore, be kept cold for a period of time following fermentation to throw out the tartrates and facilitate settling of the lees. Many of the proteins, on the other hand, are eliminated more rapidly at higher temperatures. When separated from all sediment, wines develop best at a temperature between 50° and 60° F. Chilling new wines to just above the freezing point is an effective method of quickly eliminating the cream of tartar which has not precipitated at higher temperatures.

After the various varietal wines, such as Diamond, Colobel, Delaware, Catawba, Zinfandel, Maréchal Foch, Pinot Noir, Baco Noir, Cabernet Sauvigon, etc., have been thoroughly cleared and properly aged, they are tested both analytically and organoleptically by the winemaker so that he may make his selections for blending and other future operations. Incidentally, the blending of the individual varietal wines to make commercial types of wine is an important part of the winemaker's art. Some grape varieties produce wines with one desirable characteristic, but lack other qualities that only wines of other grapes can supply. Practically all commercial wines are blends of from three to sometimes more than seven distinct varieties. In addition to blending wines of various varieties, it is oftentimes advantageous to blend older wines with younger wines in order to approach uniformity in wines produced. After the wines are blended they are stabilized and filtered. This removes fine suspended matter and stabilizes the wine to variations in temperature. The blended wines are further aged in storage tanks or casks before they are ready for final filtration and bottling.

Champagne Making. The time-honored and most famous method of making wine sparkle is that of bottle fermentation. Champagne begins as a choice white dinner wine usually several months old, and often made of grapes specially grown and selected for it. This wine is blended carefully for fragrance, tartness, and consistent quality. To it, champagne yeast and sugar are added.

The yeast induces a second fermentation, at which point the wine is placed in bottles which are closed securely to withstand developing pressure caused by fermentation, and to capture the carbon dioxide gas created. This accounts for the bubbles in the wine. It is charged more highly than most artificially carbonated soft drinks ever are. That is why sparkling wines require such heavy bottles and thick, wired-on corks. The pressure is controlled by the amount of sugar in the cuvée.

Bottles of fermenting champagne are stacked horizontally in tiers for a period of months to several years. During this time the secondary fermentation takes place. After its completion the wine ages, in the bottles and on the yeast, until its flavor and bouquet are perfected. When the champagne has reached maturity one step remains before it can be shipped. The yeast sediment must be removed. This operation can be done in one of two ways—the individual bottle process or the transfer system.

In the first method the bottles are placed upside-down on racks. Each day the bottles are lifted slightly, twisted and turned, until all the sediment has moved into the neck of the bottles. This part of each bottle then is immersed in a brine solution, freezing the wine and sediment in the neck. The bottles then are opened and pressure forces out the frozen wine and sediment. Clear champagne and the dosage—a little sweet syrup and aged wine—are added, to compensate for the wine lost in disgorging. The bottles then are corked, the corks are wired to withstand the pressure and, except for final aging, the champagne is ready for shipment.

In the transfer system the yeast sediment is removed when the champagne is filtered under a "back-pressure" of nitrogen through a filtering tank. Champagne from a large number of bottles is filtered and filled back into the bottles while the champagne's own pressure is kept constant. Just before corking, the dosage is added. The bottles then are corked and wired. Following some final aging, the champagne is ready for market.

Wine and champagne making can be described as simple. They are, after all, natural processes which run their course whether one wills it or not. But they can be complex, too. So complex that much of what goes on in a bottle of wine or champagne is a mystery to this day. We hope, of course, in the remaining chapters of this book, to clear up some of the mysteries of the magic of wine.

Chapter Two

Winemaking Equipment

Of all alcoholic beverages, wine is the only natural one—it will quite literally make itself out of grape juice. Because wine is made by a natural process it is not surprising that it can be made with the barest minimum of equipment.

BASIC EQUIPMENT

Actually, your equipment needs, to begin, will depend first of all on the nature of the raw materials you start with. If you start with fresh grape juice pressed by the winegrower or by a wine-supply shop, your problems and equipment needs are greatly simplified. If you start with fresh grapes, of course, your first task is to extract the juice. To do this you will require some type of a crusher—unless you are willing to resort to the time-honored method of crushing them with your feet.

Crusher. The usual home winemaker's crusher consists of a hopper and a pair of serrated rollers that are turned by a crank. The grapes, after the stems have been removed, are placed in the hopper and are crushed by the rollers, which are set close enough to break the grape skin without breaking the seeds. With some of the newer models available, the stems of the grapes are removed mechanically by a stemmer—a device which is either built into the crusher or attached to it.

When only a few gallons of wine are to be made, the crushing operation may be accomplished by placing the grapes, which have already had their stems removed by hand, in a tub and pounding them with a six-inch square board which has been nailed to one end of a length of wood pole and painted with hot paraffin. (For very small amounts of grapes a potato masher may be used.) But, until you have tried crushing grapes with this pestle-type

Fig. 4: Typical mechanical grape crusher used in home winemaking. It may be powered by hand or by a motor.

device, you would not believe that a whole grape in the midst of a mass of crushed grapes could resist such a great amount of pressure without breaking. When using this method, be sure not to use a copper, iron, or galvanized pail or tub for the crushing operation.

While grapes for white wine are pressed immediately after being stemmed and crushed, red wine grapes are placed in a container and allowed to ferment. The reason that these grapes are fermented with their skins is in order to get the color, or pigment, from these skins into the wine. Some commercial wineries, as stated in the previous chapter, take the crushed grapes and put them through a heat exchanger which heats the must up to 140° to 170° F. When the material is then pressed, it has a reddish-brown juice, which often has a cooked flavor if not very carefully controlled. Our personal preference is to ferment the wine on the skins because the alcohol seems to permeate the small membranes within the skins and allows those pigments to be secreted into the wine, making it a very natural dark red with true flavor.

Press. At some stage in the winemaking process the grapes must be pressed. A small hoop or basket press operated by a screw-driven piston will answer the needs of the average home winemaker. When this type of press is used, the crushed grapes (in the case of white wines), or the fermented must (for red wines), is put in cloth pressing bags, which may come with the press, or can be easily made. (This bag may be made of either burlap or canvas, and sewed and resewed at the seams with a stout cord. Many home winemakers are now using plastic screening as liners for their press baskets rather than burlap or canvas pressing bags.) As the screw is turned, the platen within the basket is driven slowly downward, and the liquid flows through the cloth bag and between the staves of the basket into a receptacle below. From the receptacle the grape juice for white wine is poured into a fermenter for its primary fermentation; while the new red wine goes into a fermenter for further fermentation and aging.

If you know anything about carpentry and mechanics, it is possible to build your own wine press. One such home wine press is described in detail in Circular 194 of the New York State Agricultural Experiment Station, which may be had by writing to it at Geneva, New York 14456. The circular contains complete instructions and measurements for construction of the home winery press.

If only a few pounds of grapes are to be pressed, a method employing a hanging cloth container for the grapes and a paddle arrangement (see Fig. 5) provides all that is required in the way of force for this operation. The rope hinge of this "nutcracker" press should be long enough so that it may be adjusted to fit the bag.

Fermenters. A fermenter is a container in which the juice is fermented into wine. While fermentation can be carried out in wooden, plastic, stainless steel, stoneware, or glass (carboy) containers, the latter are preferred because they are easy to clean and seal, and their transparency allows you to follow the progress of the wine and to exercise greater care in siphoning operations. While some old-time home winemakers feel that they can do better in wooden containers, we do not recommend these because

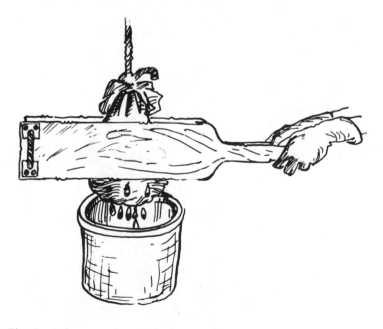

Fig. 5: A home-made pressing operation, using a hanging cloth container for the grapes and a paddle arrangement for the application of force.

they can dry up in the off season and leak, and they will need to be soaked up. They also will allow air to come through the staves and oxidize the wines very quickly, which is undesirable in the production of white types. In addition, wooden containers being organic can harbor bacteria which will certainly contribute to the spoiling of a fine white wine. (By spoiling, it is meant that certain types of acetobacter will oxidize alcohol into acetic acid, or vinegar.) Also both wooden and some plastic containers often take on undesirable flavors unless great care is taken during the clearing operation. Enamel- and stoneware containers chip too easily. Remember that wine should not be in contact with metals, except for stainless steel. Metal pickup, or "casse" as it is called, in the proportion of a few parts per million is often enough to ruin a wine.

A fermenter should have a capacity of at least 25 percent more than any one batch that you intend to ferment. The glass fermenters for home winery use are available in 5- to 25-gallon capacity sizes, but anything much over 12½ gallons is too heavy to handle when full and difficult to clean when empty. (We recommend

Fig. 6: *Typical glass fermenters.*

5-gallon glass carboys for the beginning home winemaker.) If a larger-size container is needed, which may well be the case when fermenting red wines on the skins, it may be made of stainless steel, plastic, or wood (in the order of preference). The open-end top of this fermenting vat, which should not be larger than 50 gallons, requires some type of loose covering to keep out foreign substances and insects, such as vinegar flies, from the must. The container should stand on a foundation arrangement that will raise the vat approximately 20 inches above the floor so that a pail can be put under the spigot when the wine is drawn off. Since a 50-gallon container of wine weighs several hundred pounds, the foundation should be substantial.

Fermentation Lock. While this device is called by many names —water seal, fermentation trap, water bung, air lock, water trap, ventilating bung, to list just a few—it is used for sealing the wine in a container during fermentation. We recommend its use, except when fermenting on the skins, since it saves a great deal of trouble, especially with white wines, and helps prevent the risk of having the wine turn to vinegar through contact with air.

The most common type of fermentation lock consists of a piece of glass or plastic tube about ¼ inch in diameter bent to form a loop and with bubbles blown in each upright of the U as shown in Fig. 7. The lock is fitted to a drilled cork or rubber stopper and the stopper is fitted into the container. Water is then poured into it to the level shown. The gas—carbon dioxide—formed during fermentation will build up a slight pressure and thus force its way through the water seal, but the outside air, since it is under less pressure, will not enter the container. In this way, the lock prevents air and the airborne vinegar bacteria from reaching the wine.

Testing Instruments. There are several inexpensive scientific instruments that are of great value in helping the home wine-maker to produce better wine with more consistent results. Of these, the *hydrometer* is probably the most important. With its use you can determine the amount of natural sugar in the juice; decide upon the amount of sugar to add for the desired alcoholic strength; check the fermenting process; and determine the strength of the finished product.

The hydrometer is an instrument for measuring the specific

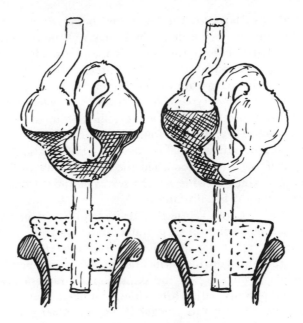

Fig. 7: A fermentation lock filled to the proper level (left) and the reaction of the water during the fermentation process (right).

gravity (the weight or density) of a liquid in which it is floated. (By definition, specific gravity is the weight or density of a certain volume of a liquid as compared with the same volume of water.) But all the winemaker uses it for is to check the amount of sugar present in the must or wine—the factor which is the basis of his principal calculations.

The hydrometer consists of a short hollow glass tube approximately ½ inch in diameter, weighted with lead shot and attached to a long spindle about ¼ inch in diameter containing a graduated scale or scales. In the United States, the winemaker's hydrometer contains either a Brix (pronounced "bricks") or Balling scale—these scales are equivalent to the percent of sugar for all practical purposes, and the numerical values are the same in both cases. They give a direct reading of the proportion by weight of "total solids" in grape juice or must; and, of course, most of these "total solids" are sugar. (When the hydrometer is calibrated in terms of

Fig. 8: The most important elements of your test equipment are the hydrometer, hydrometer jar, and floating-type thermometer shown here.

sugar, it can be called a "saccharometer.") Hydrometers are available in various sizes (the longer the spindle, usually the more accurate the reading), and you should have at least two: one in the range of −5° to +5° Balling and the other one at +15° to +25° Brix.

To work in conjunction with the hydrometer, it is wise to purchase a *hydrometer jar*, a tall glass cylinder especially made for liquids whose specific gravity is to be read. Its tall straight sides of clear glass make the reading of the hydrometer a simple task.

The *vinometer* is the only inexpensive instrument that is available to home winemakers which measures the quantity of alcohol in wine with reasonable accuracy. It consists of a slender glass capillary tube about 4½ inches long under a small thistle-shaped funnel. The capillary tube, which is graduated 0 to 25, is filled with wine through the funnel—only a few drops are required— and is then upturned onto a flat surface. The wine runs down the tube and stops at a point on the scale equal to the percentage of alcohol in the wine by volume. The instrument works simply by the variation of the surface tension of the meniscus (see page 63) and is *fairly* accurate. Unfortunately, the vinometer can only be used for *dry* wines since the sugar or high glycerol of sweet ones render it inaccurate.

Your winery should be equipped with two *thermometers*—one for telling room temperature, the other, a floating type, to indicate the wine temperature. Some hydrometers have a thermometer scale built in.

The Brix hydrometer, the hydrometer jar, vinometer, and thermometers are all delicate scientific instruments that must be kept clean at all times and stored in a safe place where they are unlikely to be broken.

Fig. 9: A typical home winemaker's vinometer.

Wine Storage Containers. White and pink wines are best stored in glass (you can use your fermentation containers for this purpose). Red wines can also be stored in glass containers and we recommend carboys for quantities under twenty-five gallons because evaporation losses (called *ullage*) and the danger of oxidation are high in small wooden casks. In larger quantities, however, these wines generally reach fuller development when stored in white-oak cooperage. (Nothing has yet been found to equal white oak as a wooden storage container for red wines, although much redwood is currently being used in New York State and California.) For home use, these hooped wooden containers, or casks, enclosed at both ends and having a bunghole in the center of their top, may range in size from five-gallon kegs to fifty-gallon barrels. While they may be purchased in some hardware and farmers'-supply stores, it is best to buy them from cooperage companies (look in the classified telephone directory under "barrels," "casks," "cooperage," "coopers") or a home-winemaker supply firm (see Appendix C).

When new wooden containers are to be used, these should be soaked overnight with a hot alkaline solution ($\frac{1}{4}$ pound of soda ash or sodium carbonate per 6 gallons of water) followed by a solution of citric acid of the same proportions, and then *thoroughly* washed with clean water three times. It may be necessary to do this treatment *several* times to bring the wooden container into a condition where it can be used. But even with these treatments excellent wines should not be stored in new barrels; these are preferably used for storing or fermenting a lesser-quality wine. After a year's use much of the undesirable bitter wood tannins will have been leached out of the wood and it can be considered to have a neutral taste. Actually, because of the difficulty of bringing new wood casks into neutrality, we generally recommend that the beginning winemaker employ old, well-washed, and clean-smelling white-oak containers, for these will not lend any foreign flavor to the wine in the first year of its making. But it is wise not to purchase wooden containers that have been charred on the inside or whose interiors have been waxed. The charring and waxing generally prevent the wine from breathing through the wood or from absorbing the beneficial tannins from the oak wood of a container. In addition, charred casks are quite difficult to clean well after using.

To withdraw finished wine from a wooden cask, a spigot, or wooden faucet, is employed and is placed in a hole drilled in one end of the container near the bottom. Wine should never be poured through the bunghole of a cask. Incidentally a mallet should be kept with the spigots and bungs so that it is readily available when needed. It is not a good idea to hit a wooden spigot or bung with a metal hammer since there is a great danger that it may split.

Siphon. Winemaking involves some transferring of the juice or wine from one container to another. At the very beginning of the winemaking process, the liquid can be poured with the aid of a funnel. (The funnel should be of good size and should be made of stainless steel.) But, once it has become wine, it should never, especially if of the white types, be poured. The reason is aeration. Not only will the wine oxidize—that is, turn brown from having picked up too much air—but it will also lose much of its flavor to the atmosphere. To prevent oxidation of the wine, it should be transferred by means of a siphon. The siphon technique also permits you to transfer the clear wine without picking up the sediment from the bottom.

For the siphoning operation, use a high-quality hose that can be sterilized without getting hard—natural rubber or flexible plastic tubing from 6 to 8 feet in length and from $\frac{1}{4}$ to $\frac{3}{8}$ inch inside diameter. If it is too small in diameter the wine will flow too slowly; if it is too large the flow will be difficult to start. If you cut notches in the inlet end of the siphon hose, this will prevent it from sealing against the side of the container. Spring-type clothespins can be used as pinchcocks on the hose. A commercial siphon unit may be purchased which includes a suction wine pump attachment.

Bottles. Finished wine should always be stored in bottles. Delicate, dry wines quickly lose their flavor, oxidize, and often turn to vinegar when stored in a larger container from which wine is regularly drawn. Then, too, a bottle is a convenient quantity for serving at the table and lends itself readily to chilling in the refrigerator. Finally, the traditional shapes of wine bottles are aesthetically pleasing.

What are the requirements of a good wine bottle? *First*, it should be of suitable size and shape and should offer the best

Fig. 10: A siphoning arrangement which employs a suction wine pump.

protection for the type of wine. The glass should be of the proper hue as dictated by custom—clear white, greenish, dark green or amber. We suggest that the home winemaker use green bottles for dry white wines. Sweet white wines should be bottled in white or very pale green bottles and the latter also are suitable for pink wines. All red dinner wines should be put into dark green bottles, ports in green or amber bottles, sherries in amber bottles, vermouths in green bottles, and sparkling wines in champagne bottles. *Second*, the bottle should be of the proper size. While the $\frac{1}{5}$-gallon size is the most common commercial container, do not overlook the possibility of using $\frac{1}{10}$-gallon bottles if the wine-drinking portion of your family is small. *Third*, it should have a simple cylindrical shape so that it stacks safely and easily. *Fourth*, if cork finish, the bottle should have a long straight neck to insure full contact with the compressed cork—this, by the way, rules out most used whiskey bottles. *Fifth*, if screw-cap finish, it should have a standard thread—28 mm for bottles; 38 mm and 33 mm for gallon and half-gallon decanters and jugs.

New wine bottles of traditional shapes may be purchased from any of the suppliers listed in Appendix C. The bottles, however, need not always be new containers. The important requirement —whether new or used—is that they must be clean. That is, they must be washed in hot water with a detergent, rinsed thoroughly several times with fresh water and then allowed to dry before use. To help in this task, mechanical bottle washers and rinsers are available which will give you sparkling clean bottles with a minimum of fuss and labor.

Corks, Caps, and Closures. When should corks, when should caps be used? A dry wine which is to be aged in the bottle for much over a year should be corked. Whether or not it will age better with a cork may quite possibly be a moot point (although we, frankly, believe it will), but of this there can be little doubt—it will be safer. It should be noted that the beginner—who almost invariably bottles his wines too early—is advised to use wood corks. A cork, as opposed to a cap, has some chance of releasing the pressure of a restarted fermentation. Also remember that cheap corks are false economy since the loss of just one bottle of wine due to a faulty cork will in most cases more than equal the apparent "saving."

Bottle corks can be obtained either with a cap for easy removal, when they are known as stoppers, or cylindrical for driving home flush. The latter type gives a neat finish to the bottle, especially when a foil capsule is used, but these corks *cannot* be inserted without a corking machine. A simple machine, which is inexpensive, consists of a chamber to hold the cork and a throat the size of the bottle neck to compress the cork as it is driven home with a plunger. Usually the straight, untapered wine cork is at least 1½ inches long.

A screw cap can be used on wine which is to be drunk up soon after bottling, or on sweet, high-alcohol wines which are relatively immune to the harmful effects of a little air. Crown caps are also suitable for short storage periods and for the fermentation stage on champagne bottles. To apply crown caps, a special inexpensive type of capping machine is required.

For champagne bottles, the plastic, reusable closures are the easiest for the home winemaker to install. (These are not suitable for still wines since they are difficult to remove without pressure behind them.) To hold the plastic or wood champagne closure in place, a wire hood should be used. It may be applied by hand or with a special wire-hooding tool.

Nothing quite finishes off the appearance of a wine or champagne bottle like a foil capsule. Available in both aluminum and lead foils, the latter type of capsule looks a bit more expensive (and is) and also requires more elaborate equipment to apply. Aluminum is very neat and can be applied with a simple rubber crimping ring.

Labels. They are an essential in some form or another. Ordinary gummed labels, obtainable at any stationery store, will do for indicating the type of wine, the variety of grapes, and the year produced. This information should be printed on the label in black (India) waterproof drawing ink. Many home winemakers make attractive and interesting labels of their own design. They give all the essential data that is contained on commercial labels and there is little doubt that the use of an original design of their own on the bottle will give them more pride, as well as pleasure, in the wine they have made.

Many of the suppliers listed in Appendix C offer a colorful selection of labels which will help to add that finishing touch to your bottle of wine. These labels as well as gummed type, if the cellar or storage room is damp, may come off after a period of

Fig. 11: Bottles with various bottle closures (left to right): screw cap, straight cork, tapered cork, and champagne—plastic and cork with a wire hood.

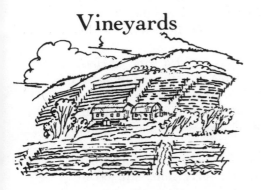
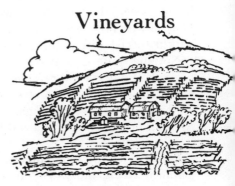

Vineyards

Vineyards

FINGER LAKES DISTRICT

FINGER LAKES DISTRICT

RED WINE

WHITE WINE

CONTENTS ⅔ QT.   ALCOHOL 12% BY VOLUME

CONTENTS ⅔ QT.   ALCOHOL 12% BY VOLUM

Fig. 12: Labels designed by home winemakers.

time. A good method of preventing this is to brush each label with a coat of transparent, quick-drying white shellac. Another way to protect the labels is to cover them with a thin layer of melted paraffin wax, applied with a small brush. This latter method has the advantage that the paraffin is much easier to remove should the bottles be reused.

Miscellaneous. As the home winemaker becomes more experienced, he will decide to include many other articles in his equipment. A few are suggested here, such as graduated cups or measuring glasses, a supply of clean old cloths, card index for keeping records of vintage data, beakers and flasks, pinchcocks and tygon flexible tubing, laboratory scale, galvanized tub for soaking bottles, hanging meat scales or platform scale for weighing grapes, a "wine thief" for taking wine samples, automatic burets, heating elements, glass stirring rod, strainer, scoop, dipper, large spoons, sterile absorbent cotton, cheesecloth, wax paper and paper

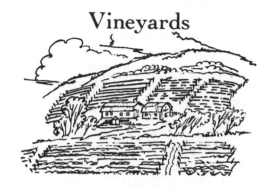

Vineyards

FINGER LAKES DISTRICT

ROSÉ WINE

CONTENTS ⅔ QT.   ALCOHOL 12% BY VOLUME

tissues, wooden shovel for handling pomace, small dolly with rubber casters for moving filled containers, paste or glue, paraffin wax, paint brush, candles, bottle brushes, plastic garden hose, refrigerator for storage of wine samples and wine in the stabilizing procedure, bung starter, and wooden cask repair tools. But let us now summarize the basic equipment needs again:

If you start with juice you need two hydrometers so that you can adjust the sugar content; a glass carboy to put it in; a cork and a fermentation lock to seal it; a siphon hose to transfer it. If you start with fresh grapes, in addition to the above you will need a crusher and a press. If you wish to make a red wine from grapes you will need in addition an open crock or barrel for fermentation on the skins. It is also important to have additional glass carboys or wooden barrels to rack into; they should be of the same size as your primary storage containers, or preferably slightly smaller.

CHEMICALS USED IN WINEMAKING

While an increasing emphasis is being placed upon the use of chemical additives by many commercial producers, we are still of the opinion that the less you do with wine the better it is. Actually more wines are ruined by home winemakers through excessive use of chemicals than by the lack of them. There are times, however, when certain chemicals must be resorted to because of deficiencies in the grapes or in the wine procedure. But remember that they should be judiciously used and not employed to correct careless mistakes of the winemaker. The amounts of the chemical to be used as given in this chapter are for the purpose of ordering them from a supplier only. Exact amounts to be used in winemaking are given in Chapters 4 through 7.

Sulfur Dioxide. This most versatile of chemicals is the only one we unhesitatingly recommend for all wines; its many virtues far outweigh its defects. It is a selective fungicide that suppresses bacteria, molds, and *wild* yeasts; however, most wine yeast cultures are very tolerant of sulfur dioxide (SO_2) and most quickly recover from a dose. Additionally it is an antioxidant that slows or prevents the browning and oxidation of wines and impedes acetification or vinegar formation.

Sulfur dioxide chemicals are available to the home winemaker in the form of a dry white powder—potassium metabisulfite or sodium bisulfite. It also comes in the form of pressed tablets called Campden Tablets.

How and when is it used? It is used in the proportion of about 40 to 60 parts per million (ppm) in the fresh juice right after pressing. The addition of about 25 ppm at the first racking and 15 ppm at subsequent rackings and 50 ppm just before bottling will do much to retain the fresh flavor of white wines and increase the storage life of any wine. There is, however, a chance that a sensitive palate may be all too conscious of sulfur dioxide's presence when found in amounts of over 50 ppm. But remember that time and agitation will reduce the amount of sulfur dioxide in the free form; therefore with patience an excess can be gotten rid of. To determine the parts per million in the use of potassium metabisulfite or sodium bisulfite, estimate from the following figures:

Fig. 13: Many home wineries have the "luxury" of a laboratory scale to measure chemicals.

Potassium metabisulfite:
    1 gram = 570 ppm in 1 quart
                150 ppm in 1 gallon
                 30 ppm in 5 gallons
Campden Tablets:
    1 tablet = 247 ppm in 1 quart
                 65 ppm in 1 gallon
                 13 ppm in 5 gallons
Sodium bisulfite:
    1 gram = 605 ppm in 1 quart
                160 ppm in 1 gallon
                 32 ppm in 5 gallons

Tartaric Acid. Low-acid grapes from the warm regions of California will benefit from its addition as they will usually clear more readily, and keep better—and certainly taste better. This is especially important at total acid levels below 0.5 percent. It should be added to the must rather than the finished wine but not in excess of 6 to 7 grams per gallon.

Citric Acid. It is found in small amounts in most grapes, but normally most of it is used up during fermentations. It forms soluble iron citrate complexes, which help prevent iron cloudiness, and it is a valuable help in stabilization after detartration. For this purpose, 1 gram per 2 gallons is quite sufficient. It may be used in the same way as tartaric acid to increase the acidity of musts. The maker of grape wines is advised to use less than 2.0 grams per gallon. The same method used to determine the amount of tartaric acid to add applies here.

Tannic Acid. Tannin, the substance which gives wines a touch of astringency or makes them "puckery," is more prevalent in the wine of red and black grapes. Thus, in the case of white wines which may be low in tannic acid, it may be added at the rate of up to 1 gram per 5 gallons. If the white wine is to be clarified with gelatin, it is wise to add previously an equivalent weight or slightly more of tannic acid.

Pectolytic Enzyme (Pectozyme). This aids in the clarification of pectin hazes if added to the fermenting juice. It is usually used at a rate of 0.5 grams per gallon. If added to the pressed must and held in this must for about a half hour or so, it will aid in a better yield of juice. This is because as pectins are reduced the "pulp" inside of the grapes is somewhat converted from semi-liquid to liquid.

APPROXIMATE WEIGHTS IN GRAMS OF CHEMICALS USED IN WINEMAKING

Chemical	¼ teaspoon	½ teaspoon	1 teaspoon
Potassium metabisulfite, powder	1.3	2.7	5.5
Sodium bisulfite	1.3	2.7	5.5
Tartaric acid, powder	1.3	2.7	5.5
Citric acid, powder	1.1	2.3	4.6
Tannic acid, powder	0.3	0.6	1.3
Pectolytic enzyme, powder	1.0	2.0	4.0
Sparkolloid, powder	0.3	0.6	1.3
Bentonite, powder	1.2	2.5	5.2
Gelatin, powder	0.8	1.6	3.3
Activated carbon, powder	0.4	0.7	1.4
Calcium carbonate, powder	1.0	2.0	4.0

All of the above are averages of measuring spoons commonly used in the kitchen. The weights are based on the material being wiped off level with the top of the spoon. If this practice is followed, you should be within 15 percent accuracy. For greater accuracy we recommend the laboratory scale.

Sparkolloid. This is a proprietary fining agent that, with the addition of bentonite afterward, usually results in a brilliant wine. Boil a small amount of wine and add ½ to 1½ grams of powder per gallon of wine to be clarified.

Bentonite. This is the most popular fining agent used in commercial wineries because it will usually clarify the most recalcitrant wine. For well-settled dry wines 1 to 2 grams per gallon is generally sufficient. Prepare as with Sparkolloid.

Gelatin. This is a common fining agent that is often used in conjunction with tannic acid. It is used at the rate of ¼ to ½ gram per gallon. Red wines are sometimes fined with this agent, especially where the wine is excessively high in tannin. (If the wine is one not excessively high in tannin, such as a white wine, tannic acid must be added when using gelatin.) Addition of gelatin will, however, lighten the color; consequently, ¼ gram per gallon is a common amount for red wines.

Isinglass. This is an organic fining agent that is occasionally used on fine white wines. When properly used it can yield a sharp and permanent clarification, especially of value with wines to be used for champagnes. Its use is fairly difficult and time-consuming, and it should only be used with white wines. We do not recommend it for general fining. If isinglass is used, tannin should be added to the wine in advance as with gelatin fining. Isinglass should not be used in excess of 3 grams per gallon.

Activated Carbon. Since it will remove much color and a little volatile acid taste, this chemical should be used as a last resort because it removes good as well as bad flavors and is incapable of reviving an already spoiled wine. The legal limit for commercial producers is about 4 grams per gallon, but the home winemaker is well advised to use less than half that amount if he uses it at all. It requires a filtration after using.

Calcium Carbonate (Precipitated Chalk). This will lower the acidity of wine, but since it acts preferentially with tartaric acid it should be used with circumspection. In no case should its use exceed 2 grams per gallon.

Yeasts. Contrary to popular belief, the so-called "wild yeasts" do not make the best wines. While these yeasts will ferment the must into wine, they and the bacteria normally found on the grapes will frequently impart their own unpleasant flavors. Two common examples are the astringent tastes of some wines and the turning to vinegar of others. Therefore, today, as previously stated, we add sulfur dioxide to the must to kill the wild yeasts and bacteria, and add true wine yeasts to do the actual fermenting.

There are two types of wine yeast cultures available to the home winemaker: (1) the dry cake or pellet form, such as the Montrachet, with which 5 grams of yeast will start about 5 gallons when added directly to must; and (2) a variety of strains on agar slants. The latter require cultivating to get enough yeast growth for more than gallon lots; they can, of course, be expanded indefinitely. The dry yeast will keep for eight to twelve months; the agar slants from three to five months if kept refrigerated.

No serious winemaker should forgo using a yeast culture of a known and guaranteed strain; it will insure more sound fermentation, a firmer deposit of lees, and, in many strains, a fermentation that will not be stopped by a cool atmosphere. Baker's yeast is *undesirable* for the making of wine. More on yeast and its use can be found in Chapter 4.

Yeast Nutrient. A chemical that assists yeast growth during the second fermentation of sparkling wines. One-half to one gram per gallon is sufficient for secondary (in the bottle) fermentation of sparkling wines.

Yeast Energizer. This will generally help fermentations made sluggish by cold, excess sugar, or yeast attenuation. It often helps to revive stuck fermentations. Since there are several yeast energizers, it should be used as directed by the supplier.

In addition to the chemicals used in winemaking, there are others that are valuable for testing the qualities of the wine. For instance, every home-winemaking laboratory should have at least 100 milliliters (ml) of N/40 iodine solution, N/10 sodium hydroxide solution and 25 percent sulfuric acid solution, and at least 10 milliliters of a 1 percent phenolphthalein solution and 1 percent starch solution. (While these solutions may usually be purchased ready-made, you may wish to prepare your own as directed in Appendix B.) In addition, you should have some diabetic test tape, one 25-ml buret for the total acid tests, and one 25-ml buret for the sulfur dioxide tests.

While some of the chemicals used in both winemaking and testing can be purchased from your local druggist, all of them, plus wine yeast cultures, may be obtained from the firms listed in Appendix C.

THE HOME WINERY

You must, of course, have a place in which to make wine. Whether this location be in the basement, laundry, garage, or even in the kitchen, the beginning home winemaker will generally have to work out some compromise between the ideal conditions and those available.

When selecting the location for your home winery, cleanliness, together with proper temperature, freedom from interference by other family activities, good ventilation, and absence of moisture are the major considerations. An area with a concrete floor with good drainage, plus running water—preferably hot and cold—is best. It is also advantageous to do the crushing and pressing outdoors on a patio or a concrete slab in the back yard. This will solve most of the cleaning problems during this messy operation.

Temperature of the winery area can sometimes determine the type of wine that you will make. Nearly all white wines require a cooler area than the red ones. The ideal temperature for white wines is between 50° and 60° F., while the red types can be made at temperatures as high as 75° F. The reason for this is that white wines are usually very delicate in flavor and bouquet, and small amounts of oxidation or browning—which are caused by higher temperatures—will harm the quality immensely. Basement temperatures, except near the heating system, are usually well suited for all winery operations. But if your basement wine cellar is too warm for wine storage try building shelves against one of the walls which is underground; seal all joints tightly and use insulating board for doors. It will keep your wine surprisingly cool. In outbuildings, such as a garage or barn, a portable heater of some type is generally needed. During storage, however, a temperature as low as 25° F. maintained for several weeks is by no means harmful to new wines.

A well-ventilated winery area is important to prevent asphyxiation during the period when the wine is fermenting and producing carbon dioxide gas. (If shielded from direct sunlight, red wines may be fermented outdoors at the same location as the crushing and pressing operations.) Proper humidity (not too dry or too wet), a means of lighting, and storage space for both the winemaking equipment and the finished wine are considerations, too, in selecting a winemaking space. Also you will want a place for testing the wine, preferably near a sink, as well as a place to keep your winery records.

The basic layout of a home winery, approximately 15 by 15 feet, shown in Fig. 14 is sufficient for producing approximately 180 gallons of wine or champagne and for storage of 12 red or white wines (5 gallons of each). The key to the illustration is as follows:

A. Window open in winter to cold stabilize wine. Open at night in summer to keep room cool. It should be screened to prevent the entrance of flies and rodents. An air conditioner may be substituted for the window.

B. Door insulated with insulation and asbestos board.

C. Frame construction with insulation and asbestos board, plus insulated ceiling to make it as heatproof as possible.

D. Drain for use in cleaning concrete floor.

E. Grape crusher and wine press on outside concrete slab. They can be brought inside after vintage season.

F. Drain ditch used in cleaning.

G. Plastic or wood containers with covers to be used in fermenting red wines on the skins. Used only during pressing season.

H. Small workbench for testing. Storage for labels, chemical agents, records, wine glasses, etc.

I. Sink with hot- and cold-water hose outlet. Can be used to clean outside area.

J. Bottling and corking area—finished wines. Storage of new bottles and supplies.

K. Bins to hold corked wines in cool dark location.

L. Twelve 5-gallon glass carboys for white wine fermenting, and later storage and finishing.

M. Three 25- to 50-gallon oak barrels for aging red wines and storage.

N. Window to pass plastic hose from red-wine fermenters to storage.

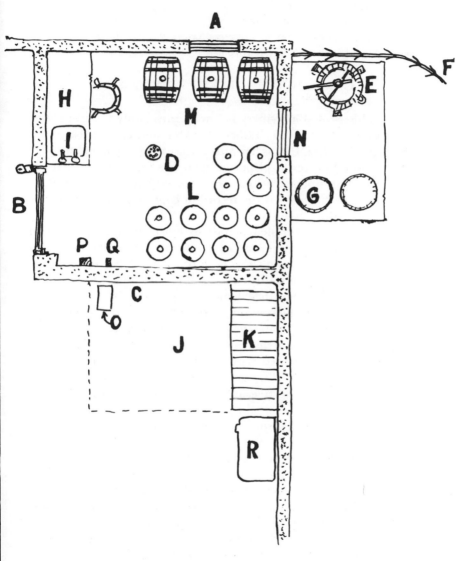

Fig. 14: The basic layout of an "ideal" home winery.

O. Small suction wine pump.

P. Room thermometer.

Q. Holder for plastic hose.

R. A refrigerator set at approximately 27° to 30° F. An old or secondhand unit is fine for this job.

CARE OF WINEMAKING EQUIPMENT

Cleanliness of your winery is important mainly to reduce contamination of the wine, rather than for antiseptic reasons. No pathogenic matter, that is harmful germs, are going to get through the fermentation process. Indeed, there are few things which you put into your stomach which are less hospitable to harmful organisms than is wine—as the record of countless millions of communicants will attest.

The cleanliness problem is not so much antisepsis, since the wine will generally take care of itself, but rather the avoidance of anything which may give an odor or foreign taste to your wine. Thus a bit of mud or a little spray residue on the grapes will have little effect on the finished wine, but just the faintest smell of vinegar or mold in the containers may prove disastrous. The same is true for detergents and soaps. It is for this reason that containers and all other items used in conjunction with your winemaking should be rinsed thoroughly. In our own cellars we use but one cleaning agent: sal soda (also known as sodium carbonate or soda ash). It is effective, readily obtainable, inexpensive, and has no odor.

Utensils such as hydrometers, hydrometer jars, funnels, measuring cups, etc., should always be washed in hot soda water and rinsed in clean water immediately after use, and care must be taken that all hoses are washed well both inside and out. Generally, glass carboys used in winemaking require only a simple washing with sal soda and rinsing out before being stored away. Sometimes, however, the wine will deposit layers of tartaric acid (cream of tartar) on the bottom, on the sides, or just below the bottom of the neck. Since these tartar crystals often are difficult to remove with a bottle brush, especially if neglected for a period of time, it may be necessary to try the use of several handfuls of coarse sand or fine gravel. If, after the grit material has been agitated vigorously against the deposit, the carboy still is not clean, there is little else you can do except to continue to use it, stains and all. Since the stains are natural tartaric acid obtained from the grape juice, they will not hurt the new wine in any way. Before using again, be sure to rinse any glass or plastic item in clean water and then let it drain.

Wood items can also be cleaned with hot soda-water solution, rinsed in fresh water, and then thoroughly dried. This procedure should be followed even if you intend to use the equipment the next day. This practice will help you to avoid attracting vinegar flies or possible molds. Also wooden parts of the crusher and presses, as well as other wooden equipment, except the casks, should be coated with lacquer so as to keep the wood surface itself dry and thus prevent mold growth.

All wooden containers used for the storage of wine are prone to spoilage and care must be taken to clean them immediately after emptying and then again just prior to the vintage season. To sterilize the cask after emptying, fill the barrel approximately half full with hot water and then add, first dissolved in water, one pound of sal soda per each 50 gallon container (proportionately less for smaller containers). Shake the barrel or roll it to mix the soda solution and then fill the container completely full with hot water. Bung tightly closed and roll the barrel occasionally. After permitting the barrel to sit at least overnight, drain, rinse with fresh, cold water. Then add a proportionate solution of citric acid, let stand for several hours longer, and repeat the rinsing operation until the water is clear flowing. (Do not use detergents in a barrel since it is difficult to remove the organoleptic traces of them.) Once the container is drained thoroughly, burn a sulfur strip ($\frac{1}{2}$ strip per 50 gallons of capacity) inside the barrel while it is tightly closed. Repeat burning the sulfur strip into it regularly once a month until the barrel is needed again. Do not store in a damp location. It is usually better to put barrels in your attic or garage than in your basement, since the latter is generally more humid.

While so holding a barrel ready for use, treat its outside surface with a coat of linseed oil. Also, keep the hoops tight. When the container is then needed after one or more sulfur burnings, fill it with water and let it soak until tight. (Even when using a new barrel, make sure it is tight—it is not nearly so distressing to see water seeping out as it is juice or wine.) Then drain and use.

The winery itself should be kept clean at all times. Any spillage of wine, grape pulp, etc., should be mopped or sponged up promptly since these materials provide ideal conditions for spoilage microorganisms that have a tendency to get into the wine and do irreparable damage to it.

HOME WINEMAKING AND THE LAW

Winemaking on any scale is subject to certain legal restrictions. Production of noncommercial wine is subject to Article 240.540 of the United States Federal Wine Regulations which states:

A duly registered head of any family may produce annually for family use, and not for sale, not in excess of 200 gallons of wine without payment of tax. This exemption does not authorize the production of wine for such use contrary to state law.

Before starting to make wine for family use, the producer must obtain two copies of Form 1541 from the Regional Office of the Alcohol and Tobacco Tax Division covering his home state.

Atlanta Office: Federal Office Building, 275 Peachtree Street, N. E., Atlanta, Georgia 30303. States covered: Georgia, Alabama, North Carolina, South Carolina, Mississippi, Florida, and Tennessee.

Dallas Office: 1114 Commerce Street, Dallas, Texas 75202. States covered: Texas, New Mexico, Arkansas, Louisiana, and Oklahoma.

Omaha Office: 2124 Post Office & Court House, 215 N. 17th Street, Omaha, Nebraska 68102. States covered: Nebraska, South Dakota, North Dakota, Wyoming, Colorado, Iowa, Missouri, Minnesota, and Kansas.

San Francisco Office: Flood Building, 870 Market Street, San Francisco, California 94104. States covered: California, Idaho, Montana, Arizona, Oregon, Washington, Nevada, Utah, Alaska, and Hawaii.

Boston Office: 55 Tremont Street, Boston, Massachusetts 02148. States covered: Massachusetts, Maine, Vermont, Connecticut, New Hampshire and Rhode Island.

New York Office: 90 Church Street, New York, New York 10007. Areas covered: New York and Puerto Rico.

Philadelphia Office: 2 Penn Center Plaza, Philadelphia, Pennsylvania 19102. Areas covered: Pennsylvania, Maryland, New Jersey, Delaware, and the District of Columbia.

Cincinnati Office: 222 East Central Parkway, Cincinnati, Ohio 45202. States covered: Ohio, Indiana, Kentucky, Virginia, and West Virginia.

Chicago Office: 17 North Dearborn Street, Chicago, Illinois 60602. States covered: Illinois, Michigan, and Wisconsin.

This form must be filed in duplicate with the Assistant Regional Commissioner at least five days before wine production is due to start in any year. One copy will be returned to the applicant to be retained at the place of production. The producer must enter on the form retained by him the quantity produced and the date of production. The form is kept so that it may be shown to any duly authorized agent of the Department of Internal Revenue if demand is made.

For information on state laws, write to your state tax bureau at the state capital.

Chapter Three

Good Grapes Make Good Wines

Only good grapes can make good wine, although bad wine may be made from good grapes if the other steps in winemaking are not performed diligently. While there are several factors in determining what a good grape is, one of the most important of these is the right variety of grapes for the wine desired.

The variety of grapes used influences to varying degrees the kind and character of the wine produced. Those grape varieties with unusually strong varietal flavors, like the Muscat, and some of the native American grapes grown in the East, make wine types as unmistakably distinct as are these grapes themselves. There are numerous other grape varieties with more delicate characteristics of flavor and aroma which are more difficult to distinguish. Wines of these grapes are also sometimes hard to distinguish when they are young, but as the wines mature they may develop noticeable differences in flavor and bouquet.

Some grape varieties produce wines of neutral flavor; others have flavors which the wine loses during aging. Still other varieties have characteristics which survive, and even are enhanced by, long periods of aging. The quality of wine is influenced not only by the variety of grape, but by whether the grape is planted in a soil and climate particularly suited to its variety. Some of the most desirable grape varieties produce poor wines in viticultural districts where other varieties excel. The degree of maturity is also very important; the grapes must be ripe enough to have a high sugar content and, for most varieties of American grapes, a low percentage of acids.

Grapes, of course, may be white, green, pink, red, purple, or blue when ripe. Some are of so dark a hue they commonly are called "blacks." They may have large or small berries, and come in bunches ranging from large and heavy to small and thin. They may ripen early or late and may be pulpy and firm or soft and liquid in texture. But the most choice wine varieties often produce small or medium bunches of grapes, and many are shy bearers—that is, their vines produce only a few bunches or are readily subject to various kinds of spoilage; thus these grapes are more expensive to produce than other types.

THE MAIN GRAPE SPECIES

There are approximately forty different species or families of grapes, from which no man knows exactly how many varieties really exist. Many viticulturists are of the opinion that all grapes are hybrids and that to carry down a single species—single variety—grape through many thousands of years untouched by any other pollen is difficult to believe. As Philip M. Wagner, one of America's leading viticulturists, mentions in a magazine article, he took a picnic lunch on the hillsides of Côte d'Or one autumn, where very little is grown except the Pinot Noir. He was amazed at the different colors and shapes of leaves and stems all bearing the same variety name—Pinot Noir.

America is credited with having a large number of the total recognized species of grapes. Four of the *main* species contributing to the parentage of most of our grape varieties are:

Vitis labrusca—the northern grape, native to the eastern part of North America. It has furnished more cultivated varieties than all other American species put together. The fruit is of the "slip-skin" type—the pulp of the berry is not firmly attached to the skin—and the vine requires low temperatures during its dormant period.

Vitis vinifera—commonly known as the *Old World Grape*. This species is the parent of practically all foreign and California grapes. Actually, most of the varieties grown of this species in the United States have been imported from Europe. The fruit is not a "slip-skin" type. The vine does not require low temperatures during its dormant period, and winter kills easily in eastern climates, except under certain conditions.

Vitis rotundifolia—its native habitat is in the southern and central sections of the United States. It thrives best where cotton will grow. This species can be recognized by its heart-shaped leaves.

Vitis riparia—the most widely distributed of any American species of grape. This species is very resistant to the grape phylloxera, a small insect which feeds on the roots of grape vines. *Vitis riparia* is one of the root stocks which was sent to France and used to reconstitute the French vineyards after they had been wiped out by the phylloxera in the period from 1860 to 1885. This species is largely the parentage of the wild grape commonly seen in many parts of our country.

While there are over a dozen more separate species of North American wild grapes which are hybridized freely with one another for various purposes and conditions, the two main wine families are the *labrusca* and *vinifera*. It should be emphasized that the *labrusca* types of the eastern part of the United States differ greatly in taste and aroma from the *vinifera* varieties grown in California. This is more than simply the difference in taste one might expect between varieties, but a general distinctive type and level of flavor that is peculiar to all the common *labrusca* varieties grown in the East. (Possibly "highly flavored" and "fruity" would be the two best terms to describe it simply.) These characteristics are due to a large extent to the type of soil and climatic conditions existing in this area. When the native varieties are grown under the conditions of soil and climate that are found in California, the flavor and aroma of the resulting grapes show little resemblance to those of the same variety grown in New York and other eastern states. From the standpoint of chemical analysis, the eastern-grown native types are, generally speaking, higher in acidity and lower in sugar content than the *vinifera* types grown in California.

Since there is such a definite difference in flavor between the *labrusca* and *vinifera* grapes, it is not surprising that there is a difference in the wines they produce. Wines made from the native types oftentimes retain more of the fruity flavor originally present at a high level in the grapes; thus the final taste of the wine is affected to an appreciable degree by the original flavor and aroma of the grape. *Vinifera* grapes, on the other hand, are, generally speaking, more neutral in taste and aroma, and the final character of the wine is more largely dependent upon flavor changes that develop during aging.

One of the greatest steps forward in grape growing, especially in the eastern part of the United States, has taken place since 1947. This has been the introduction of the French- and German-American grape varieties. These new varieties are really the best of both worlds and their development is one of the most exciting areas of winemaking, as these new tastes are finding fast acceptance with the American palate. Actually, many years ago, European viticulturists set out on the slow and arduous task of interbreeding American native vines with selected European varieties to produce new grape varieties having the fruit qualities of the best European wine grapes and the disease resistance of most American species. These are called "direct producers" and a few of the better-known hybridizers are Maurice Baco, M. Louis Seibel, Couderc, Kuhlmann, Seyve, and Villard. Most of these men developed so many varieties over the course of years that, with few exceptions, the French-American varieties are known merely by the name of the hybridizer with the original seedling number; e.g., Seibel 10878, Seibel 5279, Baco 1, Seyve-Villard 5276, and thousands of others. As it is with our native American grapes and the imported *vinifera* species, one variety will be adaptable to certain soil and climatic conditions but will be a failure when tried elsewhere.

No grape is perfect, and probably none ever will be. New combinations of characters will always be needed to suit new soils, new climates, and new purposes. Tastes are changeable and the varieties most popular in one generation may not produce wine that will be liked by the next. There are constant experiments by the grape growers and winemakers cooperating with the State Agricultural Experiment Stations to propagate and cultivate ever new varieties to produce fine wines of character.

COMMON WINE GRAPE VARIETIES

White, pink, or red wines may be produced, depending upon the availability of the proper grape varieties. In general, white wines are produced from the greenish- or yellowish-skinned varieties. (Some white wines can be produced from red-skinned varieties, providing the flesh of the fruit is not colored, which is usually the case.) Red wines derive their color, as previously mentioned, from red pigments situated in the skins of the red varieties, although a few red wines also obtain some of their color from pigments located in the flesh tissues. (The latter are termed "teinturier" varieties.) Pink wines are usually made from red-skinned, white-fleshed varieties, by removing the juice from the skins and seeds at an early stage in the fermentation, or as described in detail in Chapter 5.

Most wine grapes are unsuitable for any other use. Likewise table grapes and raisin varieties seldom make even a fair wine. There are a few exceptions. The Concord, Niagara, and Flame Tokay, for instance, are good eating and jelly grapes and can be used in winemaking. The Sultania is suitable both as a raisin grape and as a wine one. Incidentally, the Muscat varieties are "three-way" grapes, being equally adaptable to winemaking, table, or raisin use. But, as a rule, the best wines are made only from wine grapes.

Because wine preferences vary, no one can recommend varieties that will suit all palates. Those who are sufficiently interested in winemaking should test a number of varieties to find those preferred. Listed here are the more common wine grapes of the American varieties, the French-American varieties, and the California or *vinifera* varieties, and some of the principal characteristics of wines made from them.

AMERICAN (EASTERN) VARIETIES

For White Wines

Delaware. Its wine is light golden in color, characterized by a flowery-fruity flavor and a delicious aroma. Its excellent features make it highly prized by the winemaker, especially for champagne.

Catawba. While slightly tart, the flavor of its wine is pleasantly distinctive and is the basis of most eastern champagne blends.

Dutchess. The wine it produces has a pleasant delicate flavor, but the supply of this grape is quite limited.

Diamond. Its right amount of fruitiness and piquancy makes into a very distinguished high-quality wine.

Elvira. Its wine sometimes has a rather sharp aroma and a "hard" flavor, but is suitable for blending purposes.

Niagara. While not one of the best-quality wine grapes, it has been known to yield acceptable wines.

Isabella. Its wine, largely used in blends, is less often presented in its pure varietal form. Frequently it is fermented on the skins to produce a good pink wine.

Golden Pocklington. Now quite rare, its wine is of a dark straw color and its flavorful taste is of unmistakable character.

Mary. This seedling variety of the Catawba makes a pleasing wine, but it does not have as distinguished character as its parent.

Diana. Aptly named after the Greek goddess, it makes a very pleasant wine.

Missouri Riesling. Its wines are slightly better than average quality, but of no great interest.

Noah. This old-time favorite of the Midwest, yields a better-than-average wine.

For Red Wines

Concord. While not considered a good wine grape, it makes a very distinctive wine with an unmistakable flavor. Because of this, as well as its availability, it is widely used by home winemakers in the Eastern states.

Eumelan. One of the better American wine grapes, its wine is of very superior quality.

Steuben. Its wine is light, nearly pink in color, and is most delicious and interesting to the palate.

Ives. Its wine, in itself, is too highly flavored and heavy, but when blended with other red wines adds very desirable characteristics to the resulting blended wines.

Norton. One of the better native wine grapes. Incidentally, its juice blends well with that of the Ives.

Fredonia. It produces a neutral-flavored red wine of no particular distinction but is useful for blending purposes.

Worden. Many home winemakers prefer it to Concord because it has more sugar. However, it is an inferior wine grape.

Bacchus. It makes a wine which is good and which improves with age. Also good for blending.

Buffalo. A sweet grape from which a pleasant wine may be made. The color is deep burgundy.

Clinton. Its wine is rather harsh, but improves considerably with age. A good wine for blending.

Lenoir. One of the American varieties that is grown in France, it makes a good wine.

America. It produces a fine vinous (rather than fruity) wine.

Champanel. This variety makes a good wine that, with proper aging, will become very pleasant.

Delicatessen. This variety gives a wine that is highly distinctive, with a special raspberrylike aroma and the unusual combination of deep color and rather light body.

Cynthiana. Its wine has intense color, and a distinct, agreeable aroma. It can acquire bouquet with aging.

FRENCH-AMERICAN VARIETIES

For White Wines

Seyval Blanc (Seyve-Villard 5276). In our opinion this is the finest of the French-American varieties. Its wine is very delicate, of superb bouquet, and a delight to drink.

Aurora (Seibel 5279). A leading white-wine variety throughout France, this grape gives a pale, delicate wine of excellent flavor.

Seibel 9110. This variety yields a white wine of pronounced, though delicate, perfume.

Roucaneuf (Seyve-Villard 12-309). Its wine is distinctly above average, with a delicate aroma, good balance, and attractive flavor.

Ravat Blanc (Ravat 6). Producing a wine of the white Burgundy type, it is often considered the best as to quality of the white-wine French-American varieties.

Vidal 256. This grape produces a wine of delicate flavor and bouquet, plus fine aroma.

Ravat 51. This variety yields a clean, crisp white wine recalling a "true" Chablis. It is suitable for champagne, too.

Villard Blanc (Seyve-Villard 12-375). Its grape produces a wine that is neutral, soft, with good body. It is fine for blending.

For Red Wines

Chelois (Seibel 10878). A wonderful balance is found in this variety. Lightly flavored both in bouquet and taste, its color is nicely rubied and its tartness neutral.

Seibel 5898. This variety is designed for "teinturier" purposes. "Teinturier" is a term used in winemaking to describe an extremely dark wine used mostly to blend with lighter-colored ones to make them darker.

Baco Noir (Baco No. 1). Its wine is dark in color, full-bodied, and develops a bouquet similar to that of Burgundy wines.

Landal (Landot 244). A fine-quality wine grape that yields a deep-colored and remarkably Beaujolais-like wine.

Maréchal Foch (Kuhlmann 188-2). The wine of this premium-quality grape has the bouquet, with age, that recalls a good Burgundy.

Seibel 10353. It gives a good wine, though light-colored and light-bodied, which blends well with Foch and Baco Noir.

Seibel 7053. The most widely grown red-wine grape in France, giving a robust, well-balanced wine.

Léon Millot (Kuhlmann 192-2). Its wine is of deeper color and to the "experts" seems superior to its cousin Foch.

Florental (Burdin 7705). It yields a wine very similar to the world-famous Gamay Beaujolais.

Chambourcin (Johannes-Seyve 26-205). Yields a wine with little aroma but with the *sève* or body that some of the French-American varieties lack.

Colobel (Seibel 8357). This is another teinturier—its wine is not for separate use. Its color is three to five times the intensity of normal red wines.

Seibel 13666. It yields a wine of deep color and there is some kinship to Beaujolais.

Seyve-Villard 5-247. It gives a light-bodied wine of good quality and is excellent as a pink or rosé wine.

Landot 4511. This grape produces a wine of excellent quality with an agreeable aroma.

Seibel 1000. It yields a neutral wine of good quality, but it is lacking in color. This makes an excellent rosé.

Seyve-Villard 18-315. Its wine is deep-colored, somewhat astringent, excellent for blending.

EUROPEAN OR VINIFERA VARIETIES

For White Wines

Pinot Chardonnay. This, the white Burgundy grape of France, produces premium-quality wine, if picked promptly when ripe.

Johannisberger (White) Riesling. This true member of the Riesling family makes the best wines of the Rhine and Moselle types.

Gewürztraminer (Red Traminer). Its wine is fit to be compared with the best Riesling wines of the Rhine and Moselle types; and many experts consider it superior to the Riesling.

Pinot Blanc. This is the grape from which Chablis is made in France. In this country it makes a good white wine.

Chenin Blanc. Its wine is fresh, light, and fruity.

French Colombard. In character its wine is neutral and clean, pleasant and refreshing. It is very useful for blending with less-acid varieties.

Aligoté. It is often called a second-string grape when compared to the Pinot Chardonnay and Pinot Blanc, but it makes a fair wine.

Sylvaner. Its wine has a certain distinction of character and a good balance of sugar and acidity, and is usually drunk young.

Sauvignon Blanc. This variety yields an exquisite wine, rich, soft, perfumy, and oftentimes strictly comparable to French Sauternes.

Chauché Gris. Often miscalled the Grey Riesling in California, it makes an acceptable Chablis type of wine.

Palomino. Its wine is very light and flat-tasting when used as a dinner wine. It is, however, a good grape for making sherry-type wines.

Sultania. It is also called the Thompson Seedless. Its wine is almost completely neutral in character, and, if dinner wine is made of it, it should be blended with a wine having some trace of personality.

Burger. Its wine, though agreeable when made from grapes that are not too ripe, is nondescript.

For Red Wines

Cabernet Sauvignon. A Bordeaux variety, this is one of the very best of the European grapes, yielding a claret-type wine.

Zinfandel. This grape is capable of producing wine of distinctly fine quality with a brilliant color, a delicious "sweet" bouquet, rich body, and good flavor. It is a California grape.

Barbera. It has a distinct aroma, and its wine is heavy-bodied, well balanced, and when well aged has a great deal of character.

Pinot Noir. Though it has produced wines of very fine quality in this country, we feel that the physical conditions of growing this grape in Europe are better and thus the wine is much better.

Gamay. It can produce wine of distinctly superior quality.

Carignane. Its wine is characterized by good body, clean flavor, good color, and little or no distinctive character.

Petite Sirah. When young, its wine is deep-colored and astringent, with a pronounced aroma. It requires aging to be good.

Grenache. It yields a dry wine, rather short of color but of good quality, and is often employed in the making of rosé wines.

Mission. California's oldest grape, it makes only a very mediocre wine.

Refosco (Mondeuse). Its wine has good body, a very pleasant aroma which develops into bouquet with aging, and (much to the Italian taste) rather more tannin than most wines. It is useful in blending.

Ruby Cabernet. It produces a well-colored wine of moderate acidity, good balance, and neutral flavor.

Alicante Bouschet. Though its intense color offers certain advantages, it should be avoided unless there is nothing better. Grand Noir and Aramon are in the same category.

Tannat. It produces excellent wine of good body, deep color, a highly characteristic bouquet, and full flavor.

As we stated previously, it is rather difficult to recommend grape varieties because of the difference in people's palates. The following, however, are our suggestions, because of availability, and a degree of assured success in obtaining a premium-quality wine, for the beginning home winemaker:

For White Wines: Seyval Blanc, Aurora, Delaware, Dutchess, Diamond, Pinot Chardonnay, Johannisberger Riesling, Sauvignon Blanc, Semillion, and Gewürztraminer.

For Red Wines: Chelois, Chambourcin, Baco Noir, Léon Millot, Landal, Pinot Noir, Cabernet Sauvignon, and Gamay.

The home winemaker may, of course, select any grape that he wishes to make his wine from if it is available. It would, however, be rather difficult for the eastern home winemaker to get Pinot Chardonnay, Cabernet Sauvignon, or Gewürztraminer. Likewise, it would probably be equally difficult for a southwesterner to get Delaware, Diamond, or Dutchess.

BUYING GRAPES

There is little doubt that you will receive the greatest pleasure from making wine from grapes that you have grown yourself (see Chapter 9). But, if this is not possible, you will have to buy them at a vineyard (if one is nearby), or from a fruit dealer or wholesaler. It is not, of course, possible for us to give a figure as to how much you might expect to pay for your grapes. The prices vary from grape variety to grape variety, from year to year, from region to region, and often from seller to seller.

Grapes ripen in late summer and in the autumn. Earliest picking of wine grapes starts about August 15, but the main harvest is in September and October. The harvest, or vintage, is accomplished by skilled workers who carefully select and pick only the fully ripened fruit. Harvesting is an art, both as to the selection of the grapes that are ready and in wielding the sharp knives and shears. The stems and all are picked and care is taken not to rattle or strip the berries from the stems.

When to pick, as well as how, is important. As grapes mature they gain in natural grape-sugar sweetness and decrease in such fruit acids as tannic and tartaric. Most California wine grapes are picked when they reach 20 to 24 percent sugar content by weight; some eastern grapes have a bit lower percentage of sugar when ripe. For some wines in which tartness is especially desired, the grapes may be picked early, while their fruit acids are still high.

In commercial production, the winemaker is the one who specifies what special balance between sweetness and acidity he requires, and constant expert tests are made during the picking season to determine this. The home wine producer, unless he has his own vineyard, should select *fully* ripened grapes from those available at the dealer or wholesaler. Unripe grapes may not yet have developed enough of the characteristic flavor and bouquet to make a fine wine, while overripe grapes may be harboring excessive numbers of microorganisms that will later give the home winemaker problems—off-flavors, contamination, etc. To obtain optimum quality, the grapes should be crushed within 24 hours after harvesting.

When purchasing grapes directly from a vineyard, you can keep an eye on the progress of the fruit and have it picked when the stems are losing their greenness and beginning to look dry. Ripened berries usually pull more easily from their stems and the seeds are more nearly free from the pulp and generally turn brown. The pulp of a ripe grape usually has a soft texture and a slight thickening of the juice. Also the grapes are not truly ripe until they have their perfect color—green, golden, pink, red, black, or whatever color. In addition, to the experienced grape grower, one of the best guides is the full development of aroma and flavor.

Do not purchase grapes with a lot of broken skins, mold on the berries, or rotten fruit. The latter not only contains harmful molds, but is alive with vinegar bacilli—the bane of all winemakers. Thus, remember that unsound grapes either contribute undesirable spoilage organisms to the must, or give off-tastes to the wine.

It will take anywhere from ten to fifteen pounds of grapes to produce a gallon of juice, while a bushel will give up to three gallons. The variation is dependent on the variety of grape, the efficiency of the winemaking equipment (mainly the design of the crusher and press), and whether you are producing a white or red wine. As a rule, the eastern grapes do not give up their juice as readily as most French-American and *vinifera* species do. In the making of white wines the grapes are pressed immediately after crushing and the amounts produced are less than for red types. This is because for red wines the grapes are fermented on the skins before pressing; thus this operation is easier and the yield greater because the fermentation breaks down the grape pulp.

In many grape-growing regions, the juice of wine grapes is available. (Many of the suppliers in Appendix C either press premium wine juices or can suggest where they may be purchased.) As stated in Chapter 2, this eliminates the problem of selecting the grapes, and crushing and pressing them. It also permits the home winemaker to obtain the juice of some of the best wine grapes. Shipment of these juices any great distance, unfortunately, is out of the question because the juice is in fermenting stage.

To overcome this difficulty to a degree, some wine suppliers have wine grape concentrates available. As the name implies, this is juice from which the water has been removed, making it a very sweet syrup that is about 65 percent sugar. It is reconstituted before the fermentation operation by the addition of water—usually between three and five parts water to one part concentrate. (For example, one gallon of Carignane or Red Malaga concentrate gives five gallons of a full-colored dry table wine after fermentation.) While their wines are by no means premium quality, concentrates are acceptable for blending, and they do make available wine grape juices that in many cases could not be obtained by any other means. This permits the home winemaker to experiment with grape varieties from various parts of the country. Remember that experimentation with varieties and blends adds interest to the hobby of winemaking.

Chapter Four

Making White Dinner Wine

White dinner wines are usually more delicate in flavor than red, and, owing to the lack of tannin and coloring matter, defects in taste and appearance are more apparent in them. Actually, in our opinion, white wines are more difficult for the home winemaker to produce, but the rewards are much greater.

CRUSHING AND PRESSING THE GRAPES

If you do not buy juice from a supplier, your first steps in winemaking is to select the proper variety, or varieties, of fresh grapes to make the white wine from, and then crush them. It is possible, as previously stated, to make white wines from red grapes except for the few varieties which have red flesh (teinturier types), since the red pigment from skins is not readily or quickly given up except when the grapes are overripe, damaged by mold, or beginning to ferment. But this practice is not widely followed for white wines because it has no particular advantage and extra work is necessary to ensure that no red color appears in the wine. A few varieties commonly made into white dinner wine have a faint pink or red blush on the ripe berries, but this causes no problem. The grapes which are commonly made into white wines are given in Chapter 3.

In preparing the grapes for the crushing operation, they should not be washed unless they are very dirty or have lain on the wet ground. That fine, white, dustlike "bloom" on their skins is not a chemical spray, but tiny wine yeasts. However, before putting the grapes into the crusher's hopper, all culls, shriveled, insect-eaten, decayed and green fruit, should be picked out and thrown away. (An occasional bit of leaf or other minute debris common to a vineyard will do no harm whatsoever.) A mechanical crusher of the type described in Chapter 2 removes the stems, breaks the skins and frees the juice, but works so gently that the seeds remain unbroken.

If your crusher does not separate the grapes from the stems, you will have to do it by hand, bunch by bunch, before the crushing operation. As a cluster of grapes is taken from the box or basket, quickly remove all undesirable grapes, and then with a single movement pull the bunch through your hand, the grapes falling in their receptacle, the stems tossed into another. The reason for the removal of the stems is that they contain too high amounts of tannic acid, which should not be present in *large* quantities in white wines. Stems are also relatively high in ash (mineral), which may contribute undesirably to the wine.

Place the crusher over a wooden, plastic, or enamelware crock or tub. (A baby's bathtub of these materials would be fine, but do not use any metal containers, except those of stainless steel.) Then dump the grapes into the hopper of the crusher and turn the crank at about one hundred revolutions per minute, The crushed grapes will drop down into the tub or crock.

If the pressing operation is to be done in a basket-type press, put

Fig. 15: *Typical basket-type press employed for pressing grapes. Recommended time of pressing cycle for the average size used in a home winery is thirty minutes.*

the freshly crushed grapes into a strong cloth bag, which has previously been well washed and thoroughly rinsed. (In other types, the crushed grapes are placed directly in the presses—no cloth bag is employed.) Pectolytic enzyme should be added to the crushed grapes in amounts described on page 36 and then pressed after a wait of about 30 minutes. Place the bag containing the grapes in the basket portion of the press, and fold the surplus cloth so that it will not form lumps that may interfere with the pressing. Set a suitable container under the press to catch the juice squeezed out by its operation. Then apply the pressure slowly but steadily, and make sure that the full pressure of the press is employed.

On completion of the first pressing, run the platen back to its starting point, open the cloth bag, stir up the mashed grapes with your hand, and then fold the cloth as before. Press again. Repeat this process at least a third time, and if the mashed grapes still appear to contain some juice, do it again. Generally several pressings are required to extract all the juice. Overpressing, however, may extract undesirable oils from the seeds and solids from the skins. The material that is left in the cloth bag after the juice has been squeezed out is known as *pomace*. This pomace makes excellent fertilizer since it is very high in nitrogen content. But it should never be left around your home winery for more than just a few hours because it invites insects which carry acetobacter and other harmful microorganisms.

On completion of the pressing operation, a small sample of the juice should be set aside for testing, while the rest is poured into the fermenters. (It is wise to blend, or mix, the yields of all pressings of the same grape variety together.) These containers should be filled only about three-quarters full so as to avoid the possibility of overflow when the fermentation begins. (Note: If one or two drops of an anti-foam chemical—available from the suppliers listed in Appendix C—is added as soon as fermentation begins, the fermenter can be filled a little more. If you use anti-foam, be sure to follow the supplier's instruction as to its use.) Then the mouths of the containers should be wiped dry and plugged with bungs of sterile absorbent cotton or a fermentation lock.

Before you go any further, be sure to clean up any mess created by the crushing and pressing operations. Thoroughly clean the crusher and press (see Chapter 2), and wash out the pressing bags. Failure to practice sanitary precautions at this time is one of the major causes of wine failure.

TESTING AND CORRECTING THE MUST

The freshly-pressed grape juice consists mostly of water and carbohydrates. The former accounts for about 65 percent of the juice by volume, and the latter from 15 to 25 percent. (The sugars—dextrose, sucrose, and levulose—are the main carbohydrates in grape juice.) Organic acids, primarily tartaric and malic, make up from 0.2 to 2 percent of the volume, with only very small amounts of the remaining elements—tannins (mostly from the skins and seeds), nitrogenous compounds, and several minerals, including iron, potassium, calcium, and magnesium. Other acids present in mature grapes are citric, ascorbic, and phosphoric, all in *very* small amounts.

As mentioned previously, wines may be either dry or sweet, still or sparkling; wines in which the alcohol content is entirely produced by fermentation; or wines to which extra alcohol has been added. The winemaker has the choice of determining the type of wine he desires to produce. First of all he must adjust the juice to a suitable sugar and acid content. But before going further, it may be wise to say a word or two to the "purists," who feel adjusting sugar and acid by *amelioration* (the addition of water and/or sugar) is poor winemaking. True, this practice is unlawful in the State of California. It is, however, *not* a bad practice when used sensibly and is often employed in some of the finest wineries in Europe.

Testing and Correcting the Sugar Content. To check the sweetness of the juice, a hydrometer with a Brix range of $+15°$ to $+25°$ should be employed. To test for sugar with this instrument, fill the hydrometer jar three-fourths full with the fresh juice. Take the temperature of the liquid with a floating thermometer. Sixty-eight degrees Fahrenheit ($20°$ Centigrade) is the temperature at which test should be taken. For every $3°$ over $68°$, add 0.1 to the reading obtained on the Brix scale of the hydrometer; for every $3°$ under $68°$, subtract 0.1 from the Brix scale. (For more exacting temperature corrections, see page 182.)

Placing the jar containing the must on a level surface, insert the hydrometer and spin it gently. The reading should not be made until the hydrometer has come to rest and is floating freely in the liquid. When reading the hydrometer scale, place the eye slightly below the level of the surface of the liquid. Then raise the eye until the surface, first seen as an ellipse, becomes a straight line. The point where this line cuts the Brix scale, disregarding the film of liquid drawn up around the spindle by capillary action (this curved surface is known as the "meniscus"), is taken as the reading of the hydrometer. If you make your reading at the top of the meniscus, rather than at the surface of the liquid, an error

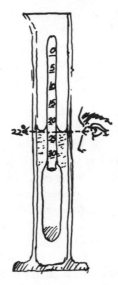

Fig. 16: Proper way to read a hydrometer.

of as much as 0.2° Brix is possible. The hydrometer should be washed immediately after use so that no undesirable residues remain on it.

Once the sugar content of the must has been determined, you can easily determine how much sugar, if any, must be added to bring your wine up to approximately 22° Brix (a desired sugar content for white juice). No juice with less than 18° Brix should ever be allowed to ferment without the addition of sugar since the finished wine will be very thin, low in alcohol, and very difficult to keep. When the sugar is higher than 25° Brix, fermentation will mostly not be carried to completion and the finished wine will be sweet. Thus, in the making of dinner wines—white, red, or pink—it is very important to keep the must in the 22° to 24.5° Brix range. (For all practical purposes, the degrees Brix are equivalent to percent sugar.)

In making up a sugar deficiency in the must, use ordinary granulated cane sugar. It should be dissolved in a small amount of the juice drawn from the fermenter for this purpose. Then pour the dissolved sugar into the fermenter and stir it thoroughly with a

ADDITION OF CANE SUGAR

Existing Brix of Juice	12% Desired Req'd Alcohol		13% Desired Req'd Alcohol		14% Desired Req'd Alcohol	
	Brix	Add per Gal.	Brix	Add per Gal.	Brix	Add per Gal.
12°	22°	.95 lb.	23°	1.05 lb.	24.5°	1.15 lb.
13		.86		.96		1.06
14		.77		.87		.97
15		.67		.77		.87
16		.58		.68		.78
17		.49		.59		.69
18		.39		.49		.59
19		.30		.40		.50
20		.20		.30		.40
21		.10		.20		.30
22		—		.10		.20
23		—		—		.10
24		—		—		.05

NOTE: *1° Brix produces approximately 0.575 percent alcohol; to produce 1 percent alcohol you need approximately 1.75° Brix.*

clean wooden paddle or glass rod for about five or ten minutes so that it is well distributed in the liquid. Then siphon off a small quantity of the juice and recheck with the hydrometer to make certain that it now falls within the desired sugar-content range.

If the must is too sweet, which sometimes occurs with some varieties of grapes, it may generally be brought into the desired range by the addition of water, or by blending it with the juice of lower-sugar-content grapes. If the acid is also low, it is usually better to leave it alone and go along with the extra alcohol. While ordinary tap water is satisfactory, no more than 15 percent of the volume of juice should be added except in certain acid situations, where up to 30 percent will improve the wine. After the water or other grape juice has been added, check the must again to make certain that it is within the proper limits.

Checking Acidity and Making the Proper Corrections. Quite frequently California grapes have a lower acidity than is considered ideal, while American (eastern) grapes are often too high. If acid is deficient in the finished wine it will be uninteresting and flat, nor will it leave a clean taste in the mouth. Juice with insufficient acid will neither ferment well nor will it clear as readily or as brightly. Wine that has a low acid content is more subject to stability problems. If on the other hand the acidity is too high, then the wine will be too tart, too coarse, too "green."

To determine the total acidity of the must, measure out 10 milliliters (ml) of the juice into a small beaker or flask and add a few drops of 1 percent phenolphthalein solution. From a 25-ml buret filled with N/10 sodium hydroxide (N/10 NaOH), permit this solution to drip, drop by drop, into the juice-phenolphthalein solution. When this solution turns pink, stop the dripping of the sodium hydroxide immediately and note on the scale how many milliliters it took in order to change the color of the juice-phenolphthalein solution. This amount is read against the total acid table. (Example, if it required 9.8 milliliters[ml] of sodium hydroxide to turn the solution pink, the total acidity of the must would be 0.735 percent.)

TOTAL ACID TABLE

GRAMS PER 100 ML EXPRESSED AS TARTARIC ACID

FOR USE WHEN TITRATING 10-ML SAMPLE USING N/10 NaOH

ML N/10 NaOH	Total Acidity	ML N/10 NaOH	Total Acidity	ML N/10 NaOH	Total Acidity
4.1	.308	9.4	.705	14.7	1.103
4.2	.315	9.5	.713	14.8	1.110
4.3	.323	9.6	.720	14.9	1.118
4.4	.330	9.7	.728	15.0	1.125
4.5	.338	9.8	.735	15.1	1.133
4.6	.345	9.9	.743	15.2	1.140
4.7	.353	10.0	.750	15.3	1.148
4.8	.360	10.1	.758	15.4	1.155
4.9	.368	10.2	.765	15.5	1.163
5.0	.375	10.3	.773	15.6	1.170
5.1	.383	10.4	.780	15.7	1.178
5.2	.390	10.5	.788	15.8	1.185
5.3	.398	10.6	.795	15.9	1.193
5.4	.405	10.7	.803	16.0	1.200
5.5	.413	10.8	.810	16.1	1.208
5.6	.420	10.9	.818	16.2	1.215
5.7	.428	11.0	.825	16.3	1.223

TOTAL ACID TABLE (*continued*)

ML N/10 NaOH	Total Acidity	ML N/10 NaOH	Total Acidity	ML N/10 NaOH	Total Acidity
5.8	.435	11.1	.833	16.4	1.230
5.9	.443	11.2	.840	16.5	1.238
6.0	.450	11.3	.848	16.6	1.245
6.1	.458	11.4	.855	16.7	1.253
6.2	.465	11.5	.863	16.8	1.260
6.3	.473	11.6	.870	16.9	1.268
6.4	.480	11.7	.878	17.0	1.275
6.5	.488	11.8	.885	17.1	1.283
6.6	.495	11.9	.893	17.2	1.290
6.7	.503	12.0	.900	17.3	1.298
6.8	.510	12.1	.908	17.4	1.305
6.9	.518	12.2	.915	17.5	1.313
7.0	.525	12.3	.923	17.6	1.320
7.1	.533	12.4	.930	17.7	1.328
7.2	.540	12.5	.938	17.8	1.335
7.3	.548	12.6	.945	17.9	1.343
7.4	.555	12.7	.953	18.0	1.350
7.5	.563	12.8	.960	18.1	1.358
7.6	.570	12.9	.968	18.2	1.365
7.7	.578	13.0	.975	18.3	1.373
7.8	.585	13.1	.983	18.4	1.380
7.9	.593	13.2	.990	18.5	1.388
8.0	.600	13.3	.998	18.6	1.395
8.1	.608	13.4	1.005	18.7	1.403
8.2	.615	13.5	1.013	18.8	1.410
8.3	.623	13.6	1.020	18.9	1.418
8.4	.630	13.7	1.028	19.0	1.425
8.5	.638	13.8	1.035	19.1	1.433
8.6	.645	13.9	1.043	19.2	1.440
8.7	.653	14.0	1.050	19.3	1.448
8.8	.660	14.1	1.058	19.4	1.455
8.9	.668	14.2	1.065	19.5	1.463
9.0	.675	14.3	1.073	19.6	1.470
9.1	.683	14.4	1.080	19.7	1.478
9.2	.690	14.5	1.088	19.8	1.485
9.3	.698	14.6	1.095	19.9	1.493
				20.0	1.500

Fine white wine can be made at total acid level of from between 0.700 to 0.800 percent. If your grape juice at this point is above the 0.800 percent mark, we would recommend adding small amounts of water to the must to reduce the acidity. Certainly no more than 15 percent of the volume of juice in water should be added. Spring or soft water is always to be preferred to hard water. The latter, however, can always be improved by boiling for thirty or forty minutes.

If after the addition of water your total acidity is still above 0.800 percent we would not recommend making any further corrections. Some of this acid will be lost in fermentation and stabilization of the wine. Ultimately you will, of course, have a rather high-acid white wine, but this would be better than diluting its delicate flavor and aroma any more with water.

ADDITION OF TARTARIC ACID

If present acid is g/100 ML	Add per gallon for .600%	Add per gallon for .700%
.300	11.4 g	15.2 g
.350	9.5	13.3
.400	7.6	11.4
.450	5.7	9.5
.500	3.8	7.6
.550	1.9	5.7
.600	—	3.8
.650	—	1.9
.700	—	—

If the must's total acidity is below the 0.700 percent mark you should add small amounts of tartaric acid before fermentation. To do this, merely dissolve the necessary weight of *U.S.P.* dry tartaric acid as indicated in the above table in a small amount of warm water, pour into the must, and mix thoroughly. Citric acid should not be added before the fermentation but may be used after the first racking, preferably after stabilization.

Addition of Sulfur Dioxide. Once the sugar and acid have been adjusted to the desired level, about 50 parts per million (ppm) of sulfur dioxide (SO_2) should be added to the must in the form of either sodium metabisulfite or potassium metabisulfite. (The amount needed for the per-gallon juice requirements can be calculated from the table on page 76.) Sulfur dioxide is added at this point in the winemaking procedure to inhibit the growth of wild yeasts which are present on the grapes naturally. The reason we wish to kill these yeasts is that they sometimes tend to produce off-flavors and often will not ferment all the way to the desired 12 percent alcohol. Often they will get part way through a fermentation and the alcohol that they have produced will inhibit them, causing what is known as a "stuck fermentation." Once a fermentation becomes stuck, it is usually quite difficult to get it started again (see page 73).

While the most efficient results of pectolytic enzyme are obtained when it is added to the must before pressing, it will help the wine after fermentation to become clearer more readily. The following table will assist you in determining how much pectolytic enzyme to use:

ADDITION OF PECTOLYTIC ENZYME

Fermentation temperature	Add per gallon white juice	Add per gallon red must
50° F.	0.45g	—
55	0.40	0.59 g
60	0.35	0.45 g
65	0.30	0.40
70	—	0.35

FERMENTATION

After the must has been analyzed and corrected, it is ready for the addition of wine yeast starter to get the actual fermentation under way. We recommend that you purchase each year new yeast starter from a reputable wine supplier (see Appendix C.) This guarantees a healthy yeast and one that will take your fermentation all the way. It also reduces the bacteria problems that often occur when home winemakers attempt to propagate their own wine yeast. However, if you do wish to propagate your own yeast cultures, we would recommend that you follow the steps outlined in Appendix B.

As stated in Chapter 2, wine yeast is available to the home wine-maker in two forms: (1) a living culture growing on nutrient agar, and (2) a dried wine yeast. The former is the most extensively used form in commerical wine production. The agar slant culture comes from the supplier in a small test tube or glass bottle plugged with sterile gauze, and it contains full instructions for use.

From such an agar slant form you develop the active liquid starter, beginning three or four days before it is needed to start the actual fermentation of the prepared must or juice. If making ten gallons of wine, for instance, you need approximately one pint of juice pasteurized several days in advance. The juice is pasteurized by heating to a simmering boil, then cooling. Be sure the pasteurized juice is *cool* before adding the yeast culture. Place in a bottle and stopper loosely with sterile absorbent cotton to avoid contamination, and at the same time to allow the carbon dioxide gas to escape. Then, after three or four days, pour the liquid starter into the juice to be fermented. Once a batch of juice is fermenting you will have an unlimited source of yeast. You need only take some of the fermenting juice and transfer it to the juice you wish to start fermenting. Yeast grows at a prodigious rate and can quickly be expanded to astronomical proportions.

While active and pure, dried wine yeast is easy to use and may be satisfactorily employed in place of a liquid starter. This dormant wine yeast is usually packed in five-gram aluminum packages under inert nitrogen gas. Each package contains enough yeast cells to start about five gallons of must. Just dissolve the dry yeast in a little warm water—warm in this case means less than body temperature; yeast is a living organism and will be killed by temperatures in excess of this—and stir it into the juice. But, once the sealed package is opened, it should be used up entirely because the dried yeast cells, when exposed to and held in air, lose their viability in a relatively short period of time.

While there are many wine yeast (agar culture) varieties that are usually available, the home winemaker is best advised to use one of the common ones such as Burgundy, Champagne, Geisenheim, or Montrachet. The latter is now also available in a dried cake form and has found good acceptance. But you should keep in mind that just because you have used a Burgundy yeast strain

Concord juice will not turn into a fine Burgundy wine. Such a miracle is not possible. A good yeast, of course, will aid you in obtaining the best from your raw materials, but it cannot convert a third-class grape into a first-class wine. But, as far as the beginning home winemaker is concerned, it is far better for him to concentrate on receiving a healthy fermentation with a good wine yeast—any good strain will be satisfactory.

Fermentation will usually be under way within twenty-four hours after the introduction of the yeast. (If the juice has just been treated with sulfur dioxide, the yeast should not be inoculated for about two hours.) If it does not start for as much as seven days, however, do not be alarmed. Remember that it is just about impossible to *prevent* it from fermenting. No two juices ferment in exactly the same way; some are often quite slow in starting—Delaware, for instance. The first symptom of fermentation is the appearance of clots of fine foam on the surface of the must, and a rim of bubbles around the edge, followed by the gradual rising and diffusion of the sediment that has settled at the bottom of the fermenter. The clots of foam coalesce rapidly, and soon there develops a thick layer of bubbles. But all the frothing and bubbling above the juice is of little value; it is simply yeast reproducing itself. The yeast which is making alcohol is working within the juice. If you have a transparent glass container this action will be quite apparent, since the juice itself will almost look as if it were boiling.

If there is too great a delay in the fermentation, it may be due to the fact that the must is too cold (below 50° F.), or that the dose of sodium or potassium metabisulfite is a bit too strong. The easiest way to increase the temperature of the must is to move it to a warmer location, or heat the home winery. If the metabisulfite dose is too great, the must should be siphoned or poured from one container to another (sediment and all) in order to aerate it slightly and thus reduce the quantity of sulfur dioxide present. Another dosage of yeast may help as well.

For the first few days of vigorous fermentation it will be quite sufficient to keep the container closed with a loose ball of absorbent cotton. Do not try to stopper it with a loose cork. Once fermentation slows down, however, you should seal the fermenter with a fermentation lock or water trap (see Fig. 7). The bottom of the fermentation lock cannot be allowed to touch the surface of the fermenting wine, and the fermentation lock must always be kept filled with water. Once the lock has been fitted in the container, run a little sealing or candle wax round where the stopper enters the carboy and where the lock enters the bung. This precaution may not be necessary, but it is better to be on the safe side. Do not forget that air can spoil any wine. It is wise to fill the container *almost* full with wine of the same variety and vintage. The ideal cellar temperature for the fermenting of white must is between 50° and 60° F. At 80° F. and above, bouquet, aroma, and flavor are damaged.

Depending upon such variables as fermentation temperature, variety of grape juice being fermented, and the type of yeast, the time that this operation will probably take to run to completion is somewhere between twelve and twenty-five days. The fermentation lock (see Fig. 7) should give plenty of advance indication as to when the fermentation is nearing its end. During the early stages of fermentation, bubbles are running through the water at the rate of one a second or even faster than this. But as fermentation slows down they become far less frequent. Later on, the water remains pushed up to one side and it may take five or even ten minutes for sufficient gas to form to make one bubble. During the very last stages of fermentation, it may take a week for one bubble to push through. It is safe to say that when the water remains pushed up to one side fermentation is still taking place. But when the water returns to normal fermentation has neared its end.

As this occurs, it is a good idea to siphon out a small amount of the wine into a clean container and measure its Balling. Balling is run the same as a Brix test. Actually, while some hydrometers are labeled Brix, others Balling, they are identical and are used in the same manner. When alcohol is in the fermenting juice and affecting the hydrometer negatively, the test is called a *Balling*.

To determine how dry the wine is and the completeness of the fermentation, use a hydrometer with a range of −5° to +5°. Pour the wine into the hydrometer jar, spin the hydrometer gently, and once it becomes still read the Balling scale. As your wine approaches 0°, it is getting dry of sugar. A wine may be completely dry at −1.5°, or as low as −2.5°.

One of the quickest ways to check for complete dryness is to use diabetic test tape. Just break off an inch or two of the test tape, put it in a small amount of the wine. If this test tape turns green, there is sugar still in the wine. If it does not, of course, you have a dry wine.

Stuck Fermentation. A fermentation which stops with fermentable sugar remaining is said to be "stuck." Some of the major causes for sticking are too large amounts of sugar; yeast reaching its maximum alcohol tolerance; too high a sulfur dioxide content; overheating during fermentation; too cold a temperature; and the presence of vinegar bacteria.

Should the stuck fermentation be caused by overheating or too much sugar added at one time, place the fermenter in a cooler location and remove the fermentation lock. Aerate the must by stirring or by pouring from one container to another. Then plug the mouth of the fermenter with sterile cotton until fermentation begins; then replace fermentation lock. If the above does not work, or the cause is due to yeast failure, add $\frac{1}{4}$ teaspoon of a yeast energizer (see page 38) per gallon of wine. Make a new yeast starter and add to the stuck wine. Sometimes, it may be preferable to blend the stuck wine gradually into another actively fermenting must. The final product is usually poorer quality than it might have been.

If the juice seems to be stuck because of vinegar bacteria, increase the sulfur dioxide level to 80 ppm and let the must sit for eight to twenty-four hours. Then follow the directions given above. If the sulfur dioxide content is too high, aerate the must and restart the fermentation as described in the previous paragraph. If the sticking is due to coldness, set the fermenter in a warmer spot.

As previously stated, it is often difficult and always a nuisance to restart a stuck fermentation. It is much better to avoid the problem than to try to correct it after it has arisen. That is, check closely on the temperature of the must and fermenting room, make sure that the proper sugar content and sulfur dioxide levels are maintained and use only a good strain of yeast.

FINISHING THE WINE

The next step is to let the new white wine settle out its sediment, or lees. As the fermentation appears to cease, the containers should be filled *completely* full with wine of the same variety and vintage. When this is done, wipe the mouths of the fermenters clean and then install the fermentation locks again just in case the wine may still be fermenting a bit. If you seal the container at this point, the fermentation gases may build up sufficiently to explode the vessel. Store the containers in a cool spot (preferably between 50° and 55° F.) in your winery for about two weeks, but be sure to check them *at least* once a week to make certain that they are full right to the very top. Not to keep them full is to run the risk of spoiling the wine. Once you are sure that the fermentation has

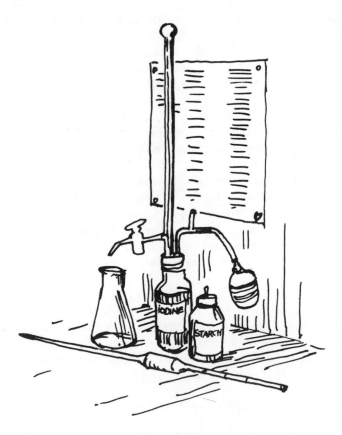

Fig. 17: *Equipment recommended for the sulfur dioxide test.*

ceased, the lock may be removed and a solid stopper or bung installed. All junctions can be sealed with wax or paraffin.

Sulfur Dioxide Test. Before racking the wine, it is a good idea to check the level of sulfur dioxide. If the wine is completely dry, add the proper amount of potassium or sodium metabisulfite to bring the sulfur dioxide level back up to 25 to 30 ppm free. This will kill any bacteria and allow them to precipitate to the bottom with the rest of the fermentation lees. The test for free sulfur dioxide is made as follows: Pipet 20 ml of wine in a flask and add several drops of 25 percent sulfuric acid solution and several drops of a 1 percent starch solution. Then fill a 25-ml buret with N/40 iodine solution and let it drip, drop by drop, into the flask. When the liquid turns blue-black in color, stop the dripping and note the number of milliliters of iodine used. You will then be able to determine the amount of free sulfur dioxide from the following table (example: 1.0 ml equals 40 ppm of SO_2 in the wine):

SULFUR DIOXIDE—PARTS PER MILLION
(USING 20-ML SAMPLE)

ML Iodine	SO_2	ML Iodine	SO_2	ML Iodine	SO_2
0.1	4	1.5	60	2.9	116
0.2	8	1.6	64	3.0	120
0.3	12	1.7	68	3.5	140
0.4	16	1.8	72	4.0	160
0.5	20	1.9	76	4.5	180
0.6	24	2.0	80	5.0	200
0.7	28	2.1	84	5.5	220
0.8	32	2.2	88	6.0	240
0.9	36	2.3	92	6.5	260
1.0	40	2.4	96	7.0	280
1.1	44	2.5	100	7.5	300
1.2	48	2.6	104	8.0	320
1.3	52	2.7	108	8.5	340
1.4	56	2.8	112	9.0	360

Once you know the amount of sulfur dioxide present, use the following table for the correct amount of potassium or sodium metabisulfite to add to bring the SO_2 up to the proper level:

ADDITION OF POTASSIUM OR SODIUM METABISULFITE

If SO$_2$ content is	Add per gallon to reach 30 ppm	Add per gallon to reach 50 ppm	Add per gallon to reach 80 ppm
0	.30 g	.50 g	.75 g
10	.20	.40	.65
20	.10	.30	.57
30	—	.20	.50
40	—	.10	.40
50	—	—	.30
60	—	—	.20
70	—	—	.10
80	—	—	—

NOTE: *Roughly 0.50 grams per gallon will raise SO2 content to 50 ppm.*

The use of sulfur dioxide is practically essential in handling white dinner wines. Its rational use protects these wines against a too-dark color, bacterial disease, and an oxidized, sherry-like flavor and aroma. But since sulfur dioxide is constantly being dissipated by volatilization, oxidation, and the like, it must be replenished at regular intervals, though in lesser quantities as the wine becomes biologically more stable with age. Also when proper sanitary precautions are employed in crushing, pressing, fermenting, storage, and racking, sulfur dioxide is never needed in objectionable amounts. In addition, the cooler the cellar, the less acid the wine, the larger the container, the smaller the amounts of sulfur dioxide necessary. Remember that small doses repeated as necessary are preferable to a single large dose.

Racking. The racking of wine is an exceedingly simple procedure and, as previously mentioned, consists merely of drawing the wine out of one container and putting it into another. This operation is very important to obtain a clear, stable, and mellow-tasting wine. Once the agitation of the fermentation has stopped, then the bits of skins, stems, dirt, and dead yeast will slowly start settling to the bottom as sediment—called *lees.* When dead yeast decomposes, it gives off musty flavors. Thus, the wine should be racked, or taken from its lees, before this can happen.

After about two weeks of storage and after completion of fermentation, the new wine should be siphoned—it is next to impossible to pour without stirring up the sediment—off its lees into a clean container. Obviously, because of the lees, you are going to end up with a little less wine than you started with. (The lees are thrown away.) You must accordingly rack into a smaller container or make up the shortage with a similar-type wine. Since one of the most important rules in winemaking is to protect the wine at all stages from air, it is of *prime* importance that the containers be kept completely full. We repeat, keep your containers full and keep them sealed.

After the *first* racking, it may be necessary to use the air lock, since this operation sometimes restarts fermentation. When this secondary fermentation has ceased—usually in a couple of days— replace the fermentation lock with a solid cork or stopper. Test for pressure each day for a few days by easing out the cork. Once you are convinced that there is no formation of gas, all junctions may be sealed with wax or paraffin.

The management of the siphon is quite easy. It can be started by applying positive pressure over the liquid at the inlet end of the siphon hose, or by negative pressure (suction) at the outlet end. The original container (the inlet end) must always be higher than the new container (the outlet end); it is inadvisable to move

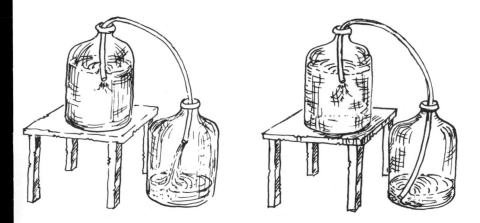

Fig. 18: Proper arrangement of equipment for the siphoning operation. (Left) Start of siphoning operation. (Right) When wine begins to flow, submerge tube into wine to prevent aeration.

the container with the settled wine since the lees are too easily disturbed. Incidentally, best results are obtained when the difference of height is not too great. When the difference is great, the wine entering the hose forms a vortex which markedly disturbs the sediment. The inlet end should be lowered gradually, just under the surface of the wine, while approaching the deposits. This will also help prevent disturbing the lees. The hose can be held in position in the neck of the container by a clip-type clothespin.

To keep aeration at a minimum, add potassium or sodium metabisulfite to bring the free SO_2 to 30 to 50 ppm. Start the siphon flow and after a pint or so of wine has flowed, shake the new container so that the chemical will dissolve and be dissipated. Care should be exercised in sucking on the siphon so that the liquid draws the first time; if not it is quite easy to disturb the carefully settled lees with the sudden backflow. This can be alleviated by placing the end of the hose in the original container near the top until the flow is definitely started. The wine should not be allowed to run down the side of the new container, but the hose should be immediately immersed in the wine and the container be allowed to fill without splashing. If a little sediment is picked up on one racking it will do no harm and you will most likely be able to get rid of it on the next. As the empty container nearly fills, slowly press the hose between the finger and thumb in order to cut off the flow slowly rather than with a jerk. Sudden stoppage often stirs up the sediment. When you rack, the siphon hose and the new container must be clean and sterile. There must be no foreign odors whatsoever in your equipment. The racking operation should be repeated three or four times during the winter and spring.

If, during the racking operations, you want to check the "rough" alcohol content of your wine, a hydrometer and your winery records (see page 91) are all that are needed. Since it is the sugar which makes the alcohol, if we know how much sugar has been used up then we have a good estimate of the alcohol produced. If the fresh juice reads 22° Brix before fermentation had started and presently reads 17° Balling then we have used about 5° Brix in the production of alcohol. Roughly about 2.9 percent alcohol has been created if 1° Brix produces 0.575 percent alcohol. However, this method of alcohol calculation becomes increasingly more inaccurate because of the negative effect of alcohol on your hydrometer.

Between rackings the containers should be tightly stoppered or sealed, completely filled, and kept in a cool location. If any time during your inspections of the winery you note any bubbles or flowerlike formations forming on the surface of the wine, check the sulfur dioxide content immediately, and, if not 20 to 30 ppm free, adjust it to that level.

Before clarifying, or fining, the wine, you *may* wish to add a small amount of powdered tannic acid to give it a touch of astringency, which all lovers of a very dry wine enjoy. The tannic acid helps also to impede oxidation and aids in maturing of the wine. However, do not use more than approximately 2 grams per 10 gallons, or ⅕ gram per gallon. Mix the acid powder with a small amount of wine and then pour into the storage container.

Fining. This is the process in which you assist the wine, by the addition of various materials (called *finings*), to precipitate out all traces of suspended matter and thus to become perfectly clear and have "bottle brightness." Most healthy wines will generally clear themselves in *time.* If your wine is not becoming brilliantly clear by late spring, it should be fined before the warm weather. A quick test to judge the necessity of this operation is to hold a lighted match or candle, in a dark room, behind the glass container holding the wine. If the flame is sharp and clear, the wine does not need fining, but if the flame is fuzzy, it should be done.

Formerly, Spanish clay, isinglass (fish glue), gelatin, egg whites, and various casein products were used as finings. While these are still highly recommended clarification agents, the home winemaker usually makes use of two easy-to-use materials: Sparkolloid and bentonite.

Using the Sparkolloid first, take approximately 50 milliliters of wine of the type you wish to clarify, and put into a vessel that can be heated. Then add 2½ to 3 grams of Sparkolloid. (This batch will be enough to clarify approximately 10 gallons of wine.) Stir the Sparkolloid into the wine as it is being heated to its boiling point; once this is attained, pour the proper amount of the Sparkolloid solution into the container of the wine you wish to clarify.

The same procedure is followed immediately, but this time

bentonite is employed at a rate of 10 grams to 10 gallons of wine. The bentonite is dissolved in 50 milliliters of wine, which is brought to a boil and then put into the container of the wine to be clarified. After the two fining agents have acted for several days, siphon off the supernatant liquid on top of the clarification lees, throwing away these lees. Actually, through racking and fining the wine you will lose about 10 to 15 percent of the original quantity.

Stabilization of the Wine. The next step in the winemaking process is the stabilization of the wine. First, the wine should be placed in containers that will fit into your winery refrigerator. Set at a temperature of 27° to 30° F. The wine should be left in this refrigerator for not less than a month in order to precipitate its cream of tartar or potassium bitartrate crystals. (If the white wine is not given this chilling period, these crystals, often called *gravel* or *sand* by winemakers, may develop subsequently in the bottle, and the wine may also become cloudy when chilled.) After the chilling period of a month has been completed, siphon off the supernatant liquid from the cream of tartar crystals and throw these crystals away.

If you have a filter arrangement in your home winery this is the point in the process where it would be employed. Several systems are discussed in Chapter 5, and the techniques described would hold good in white wine making, too.

Just before storing the wine for its final aging, you may wish to add a small amount—up to 5 grams per 10 gallons of wine—of citric acid in order to help stabilize the wine. If your wine is already excessively high in acid, it would be wise not to add any citric at all.

Once again the sulfur dioxide level should be carefully checked to be sure that it is from 20 to 30 parts per million. After this has been done, the wine should again be placed away in cool storage and allowed to remain for one or two months. If, at the end of this time, the wine is brilliantly clear and the aroma is perfectly clean, it is ready for bottling. If your wine is not bottle bright as yet, do not worry. Just set it back in storage and let it clear naturally before bottling. This may require six or eight months, but the extra needed time goes along with the production of a high-quality white wine.

BOTTLING WINE

The bottling operation begins with *thoroughly* clean bottles; we cannot overemphasize this because nothing seems to pick up alien odors and flavors as readily as good wine. Therefore, all bottles must be washed.

New bottles are easily washed and then rinsed out with scalding water. Used bottles must be washed with a suitable detergent solution—soda ash, trisodium phosphate, or metaphosphate solution. Follow carefully the manufacturer's directions for use of the detergent selected. Bottles should be washed until free of all adhering foreign matter. A good long-handled bottle brush will help with this task. But, if there is any stubborn adherence of foreign matter which the brush cannot remove, try cleaning the bottle by putting in a handful of small gravel or coarse sand, and shake vigorously backward and forward, sideways, and up and down. If this fails, throw the bottle away. There are mechanical brushes and bottle washers available and they may be purchased at winemaker's supply houses. Incidentally, when planning to save your

Fig. 19: Two types of mechanical bottle-washing brushes.

wine bottles for reuse, rinse them out with hot water immediately after they have been emptied. (Never let a bottle stand around with a bit of wine in it, no matter how little.) Then store them upside down, and, when you are ready to use them again, scalding with hot water is all the care they will generally need.

After being washed, the bottles must be thoroughly rinsed. This is invariably done in the wrong manner; water from the tap is permitted to run into the bottle until it overflows, which is almost totally ineffective. The proper way to rinse a bottle is upside down, with the water introduced by a nozzle or jet stream, which hits the bottom of the bottle first and flows down the sides; in this way at every instant the bottle is being flushed by clean water. After rinsing there should be no odor whatsoever in the bottles. They should be stacked upside down so that all the water may drain out before use.

If corks are to be employed, they must be prepared before they are used. As was stated in Chapter 2, you need a special corking device to insert the corks; but first they must be softened. This is done by soaking them in lukewarm water until soft. After softening, drain thoroughly and be ready to use them immediately before they harden again.

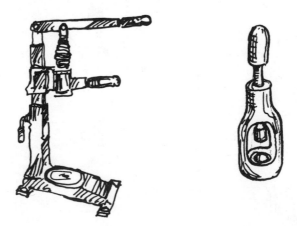

Fig. 20: Examples of corking devices used by home winemakers: (left) bench type—cork is inserted with one lever, compressed with the other; (right) hand corker—lever drive and lever squeeze.

To fill the bottles, siphon the wine from the storage container, being careful not to pick up any excessive oxygen by splashing the wine into the bottles. (It is needless to say that the sulfur dioxide level during this operation must be kept at a minimum of at least 20 to 30 parts per million.) After the bottle is filled to within a half to three-quarters of an inch from the bottom of where the cork will be, the cork itself is then inserted and driven to a level just below the top of the bottle by means of the corker. Once the bottles are corked they should be labeled. These labels should contain such information as the grape variety, vintage date, and when the wine was bottled. Be sure that the bottles are stored on their side in order to keep the cork wet and pliable on the inside. If the corks are permitted to dry out, air will be allowed inside the bottle and will oxidize your fine white wine.

Should you wish to have a slightly sweeter white wine, such as a Sauterne, a slight amount of sugar may be added to the wine just before it is bottled. Make sure, however, that the sugar is thoroughly dissolved and that the sulfur dioxide level has been raised to 60 to 80 parts per million. The addition of sugar just before

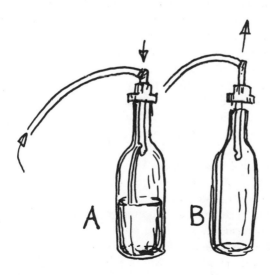

Fig. 21: Siphon and bottle filler. The filler is inserted in the bottle and pressed down and the valve automatically opens; release pressure and valve closes.

bottling gives the wine more ingredients from which micro-biological life may attack and spoil the wine. Also, the addition of sugar makes the advent of another fermentation a distinct possibility. For these reasons, we usually recommend that the *beginning* home winemaker stay strictly with dry wines.

Should you drink the wine a day or two after bottling, the chances are that the results will be rather disappointing, especially if it is of a premium-quality type. The wine will usually taste flat and uninteresting. Since the bottling operation inevitably involves some degree of aeration, some of the wine's flavor will be dissipated; it will take perhaps a month or more for the wine to recover fully. When bottled, your white wine will generally have an age of only approximately eight to twelve months. The reason for bottling white wines young is that they are then lighter in color, higher in fermentation aroma, less in bouquet, and fresher and fruitier in taste. We usually recommend that white wines be consumed in your home within the next year or two because of the likelihood of oxidization or browning of the wine if kept too long.

It is a good idea to give the bottles a visual inspection from time to time to be sure that your white wine remains sound. Should it precipitate small amounts of sediment to the bottom of the bottle, do not worry. Some of the wines sold commercially in this nation carry small amounts of sediment. In fact, your wine with its little sediment may well be finer than many commercial wines, because these commercial types have been run through so many steps of production to prohibit or prevent this precipitation that much of the quality has been lost. When serving wine with sediment, carefully decant it; should a little of this precipitated sediment get into a glass, do not be concerned. It is not poisonous in any way and will not hurt you in the least, except that oftentimes it has a bitter or astringent taste.

If mold should form on the exposed end of the cork do not be alarmed; it is completely harmless and will not affect the wine. It is because the corks may be unsightly that commercial wines have capsules over them. The home winemaker, of course, can use foil capsules, too. We do not agree with some winemakers who indiscriminately seal their corks in place with paraffin or sealing wax to prevent mold and moisture from affecting the cork and possibly damaging the wine. In some instances, where storage in a damp location is necessary, this *may* be acceptable, but generally it is better not to seal the corks in their bottles as this prevents the wine from "breathing." Natural wood corks are organic and porous, which permits the residual sulfur dioxide gas to pass out and small amounts of oxygen to pass in. This, of course, promotes further aging and maturity.

WINE RECIPES

Detailed wine recipes that often appear in winemaking books and magazine articles are of necessity both inaccurate and misleading. These recipes fail to take into consideration that two of the important qualities of grapes—sugar and acid—vary not only from vintage year to vintage year, but from region to region, and, indeed, vineyard to vineyard. Thus, when a recipe directs flatly, "Add 2¼ pounds sugar and 1½ pints water," it is only an approximation, and often a very *poor* approximation. Should a wine from such a recipe turn out well it should only be considered good luck rather than intrinsic soundness.

In this book, it is our intention to give the would-be winemaker a full understanding of the fundamentals of the process. The blind following of recipes or your neighbor's advice will teach you very little and may, indeed, give you troubles. Actually, there is only one way to make good wines year in and year out: you must develop good judgment and skill in measuring everything that goes into the wine. You must keep records; you must compare your wines not only with others but, occasionally at least, with the best. Remember that winemaking is not fool-proof. But therein lies its fascination; it is this which makes it such an enduring passion. Rather than a recipe, the following is a summary of the steps necessary in making a fine white dinner wine:

1. After purchasing grapes of the desired variety or varieties, stem and crush them, making sure that all berries are broken, but do not crush seeds. Add enzyme. Press and prepare to ferment immediately; prevent contact with metals. Collect juice in fermenting container; a glass carboy is ideal. The container should be filled only three-quarters full. Add 50 ppm of sulfur dioxide.

2. Test the must for sugar and acid content and make proper

adjustments. Add yeast and stir thoroughly. Plug loosely with sterile cotton.

3. When violent fermentation has slowed down, usually in three or four days, attach water trap. If possible, move wine to cool area—50° to 60° F. Add makeup wine so that container is almost full.

4. When fermentation has about stopped—this may be from about twelve to twenty-five days—solids will begin to settle. Keep container full; keep water in fermentation lock. This is the stage when the beginner gets careless—a loose cork, a partially filled jug, or an empty fermentation lock will quickly spoil your wine.

5. After two weeks or so of aging, rack off the wine from the lees. That is, carefully siphon off clear wine into another container to which has first been added 30 ppm of sulfur dioxide. Fill container, if necessary, with similar-type wine. Replace fermentation lock—racking sometimes restarts fermentation. After a couple of days replace with a solid cork or rubber stopper.

6. Rack three or four times before the onset of warm weather; keep sulfur dioxide at 20 to 30 ppm. level. Be sure the containers are kept full and in cool location.

7. Add tannic acid if needed. Then use fining agents (Sparkolloid and bentonite) to clarify the wine.

8. Stabilize the wine by giving it a chilling period in a refrigerator; siphon off clear wine from top of the cream of tartar crystals. Citric acid is also sometimes used to help in the stabilization of wine. Wine may also be filtered if equipment is available. Before the final aging storage, be sure that sulfur dioxide level is kept at 20 to 30 ppm.

9. When wine is brilliantly clear, it may be bottled. After bottle aging, the wine can be drunk and enjoyed.

The above are only the basic steps in the making of white wines. One can see the many variables that exist for a winemaker, not only the variety of grapes that he is using, but the temperature variances, the many different types of equipment, materials, and other items that a winemaker has at his disposal to make his wine distinctive.

Chapter Five

Making Red Dinner Wine

For the beginning home winemaker, red wine production is perhaps the most practicable because it seldom fails. Apart from the obvious differences in color, we generally expect red wines to be more astringent and a little more full bodied than the white wines. This is a consequence of the whole grape's being part of the initial fermentation.

FERMENTATION ON THE SKINS

The grapes are stemmed and crushed as in the making of white wine and collected in a crock or tub. (Some winemakers clamp the crusher directly over the open fermenting vat so that juice and pulp may run directly into the container.) Once this operation is completed, remove a small sample of the juice and set it aside for use in testing for sugar content. Fill the fermenting vat approximately three-quarters full with the crushed grapes. Then, to this must, add a dose of potassium or sodium metabisulfite in sufficient amount to bring its sulfur dioxide level up to at least forty parts per million free (page 76). When the required amount of the chemical has been stirred into the must, cover the open top of the fermenter with a piece of clean cheesecloth to keep out fruit flies and dust.

With the $+15°$ to $+25°$ range Brix hydrometer, determine the sugar content of the juice in the same manner as for white wine, and calculate the amount of granulated cane sugar required to adjust the juice to $22°$ Brix sugar content, or whatever you desire.

The acidity test is also conducted in the same manner as for white wine, except that the end point will come when the juice becomes blue or green rather than pink. Red wine seldom requires the addition of tannic acid because the skins and seeds contain this chemical. Some people seem to prefer a red juice with a range of 0.80 to 1.00. If the amount of acid is too great, the juice may be diluted with water. If too low, add a proper amount of powdered tartaric acid.

After letting the must stand for about two hours, add the liquid yeast starter. Keep the fermenting vat in a fairly warm place with the temperature preferably between $65°$ and $75°$ F. As the carbon dioxide formed is liberated, the skins will separate from the juice and form a floating cap. At least twice a day this cap should be punched down into the liquid. This aerates (not as critical in reds as in white wines) the whole vat, thus recharging the yeasts and helping to make the fermentation complete. This important procedure also inhibits the bacteria from growing in the cap and it helps in the extraction of color. An eight-inch-square flat board nailed to a clean stick can be used for punching the cap down. Under no circumstances should the foam or must be allowed to run over the sides of the fermenter, since it will acetify, draw flies, and create an unsanitary appearance. Once the fermentation has shown signs of slowing down, a loosely fitting lid, with several holes drilled in it, may be placed on top of the fermenting vat and a piece of cheesecloth thrown over it.

Probably the most favorable condition for fermentation is proper temperature. Extremes of cold or heat can paralyze desirable wine ferments, at least temporarily. While the home winemaker can usually control the temperature of his winery area fairly easily, since it can vary anywhere from 55° to 75° F., the temperature of the must should be carefully watched. In larger quantities, it will rise considerably during fermentation, but it should not be permitted to go above 90° F. You may control the fermentation temperature to some degree by controlling the temperature of your winery area and by keeping the fermenter sizes under twenty-five gallons capacity. The removal of the vat lid will also help; however, be sure to keep the vat covered with a piece of cheesecloth. The temperature reading of the must in the fermenter should be taken each time just after the cap has been punched down thoroughly.

As with white wines, the course of the fermentation may be followed by daily hydrometer readings. When the reading is between +2.0° and −1.0° Balling (which usually requires anywhere from five to ten days, depending on the temperature at which the fermentation proceeds), most of the grape sugar will have fermented. It is now time to separate the skins from the wine. During this primary, or first, fermentation, the new wine obtains from the skins its color and much of its quality, not to mention the fact that all of the wine's alcoholic strength is determined by the activity of the yeasts during this period. In taking the Balling degree, a hole is punched in the cap after it has been punched down and a dipperful of the fermenting must is taken. If it contains much pulp and skins, it should be strained. A kitchen screen-type strainer will suffice; or a layer of cheesecloth will do. The must is then poured into a hydrometer jar and a hydrometer is floated in the liquid and read at the level of the liquid (see page 63). Also the temperature of the must in the hydrometer jar is taken. From the temperature correction table in Appendix B, the suitable temperature correction is made and proper Balling degree obtained.

When the time comes to separate the cap from the wine, the cap should be skimmed off and placed in a separate receptacle. The new wine remaining in the fermentation vat is drawn off and strained through washed cheesecloth to remove the seeds and other matter which may have settled to the bottom. The thick cap, plus any remaining pulp and skins, is placed in the cloth bag of the basket press and pressed. When all the juice has been pressed out that will come, reopen the press, loosen up the pomace with your hands, and give it another pressing. Then mix the pressed wine with the strained liquid taken from the fermenter vat. If a press is not available, the must cap can be put in cheesecloth and squeezed by hand.

The partially-fermented juice should then be transferred to a glass or wooden container, which should be filled to about 90 percent of its capacity. A fermentation trap should be attached. It may take several days for the residual sugar to ferment. When fermentation subsides, fill the container completely with wine— preferably of the same type, but in any case with similar wine of good quality. We cannot overly emphasize the importance of keeping the container completely filled at all nonfermentative times to avoid spoilage. When glass or plastic storage containers are employed, some home winemakers add a *few* white oak chips or shavings for developing fuller flavor, but this may prove to cause a problem in later stabilization efforts. Place the filled red

FERMENTATION RECORD
VAT #3

Grape Variety *Baco Noir* Amount: 100 gallons		Sugar Content 18° Brix Total Acid 0.90	
Date	Operation	Balling	Temp. of Must
9/1	Grapes crushed, vat filled, SO₂ added	18°	65° F.
9/1	Sugar and yeast starter added	22	65
9/2	First signs of fermentation	21	67
9/3	Active fermentation	18	70
9/4	Active fermentation	14	75
9/5	Active fermentation	11	79
9/6	Active fermentation	7	83
9/7	Active fermentation	3	85
9/8	Active fermentation	1	84
9/9	Active fermentation, must pressed, wine in storage	−1	81

NOTE: *A smaller amount of must would not indicate as much temperature variance as that shown above.*

wine storage containers where the thermometer will hover between 65° and 75° F.

Fermentation Record. A prerequisite common to all winemaking is that of record keeping. This is especially important during fermentation. The simple form shown on the previous page is easy to follow for this operation.

Such a record should be kept at or attached to the fermenter containing the material under fermentation and later be brought forward for the succeeding stages of racking, blending, fining, aging, etc. Actually, a permanent record is preferred, as you may wish to refer to it to explain the anomalous character of the finished wine.

FINISHING THE WINE

In the time period between the end of November and mid-December, the new wine will start to lose some harshness and turbidity and may even become fairly agreeable to taste and clear to the eye. In commercial wineries, this is the time when they make very careful analysis of the wine's true composition. While most home winemakers do not make these tests, they should at least know about them and understand their purpose. Incidentally these tests—alcoholic percentage, total acidity, and volatile acidity—are performed on white wines as well as red.

Checking Alcoholic Percentage. You can generally approximate in advance the alcoholic content of your wine. For instance, one convenient formula for estimating the alcohol content to expect in a dry wine is: degrees Brix of the crushed grape (original unfermented must) times 0.575 equals alcohol in percentage by volume after fermentation. This estimate corrects for the conversion of some sugar to other products, takes into account the extract, and expresses the alcohol in the usual wine units. (*Extract* is an expression of total solids dissolved in a wine. If a wine is dry, the extract would be color pigments, glycerols, etc., contributing up to 3.0 percent of a wine's composition. A sweet wine would contain more solids—a higher extract—because of the sugar solids dissolved in it.) Therefore, grapes testing 20° Brix can be expected to give off about 11 percent alcohol by volume or numerically slightly more alcohol than half the "sugar" (dissolved solids) in the proper units. (*Proper units* are expressed in same manner as for a Brix or Balling test—in degrees—or, for all intents and purposes, a percentage.) A dry wine is normally about +2.0 extract regardless of alcohol content. Extract, as opposed to Balling, does not take into consideration the negative effects of alcohol on specific gravity.

There are times, however, when it may be desirable to check the predicted alcoholic percentage against an actual test. There are three ways of checking the alcoholic percentage: distillation procedure, ebullioscope method, and with a vinometer.

Distillation procedure. The following equipment is needed: one 1,000-ml Erlenmeyer flask, 200-ml Kohlrausch volumetric flask, Liebig condenser with its support, hydrometer with Tralle scale, hydrometer jar, a source of heat, a cold-water connection to the condenser, and a drain from the condenser.

To start this check, rinse the volumetric flask with a sample of the wine to be tested. Then fill the volumetric flask with the wine to the blue line inside the container. The contents of the volumetric flask are now emptied into the Erlenmeyer flask of the alcohol distillation apparatus. Rinse the volumetric flask at least three times with a few milliliters of distilled water, repeatedly putting the distilled water contents into the Erlenmeyer flask along with the wine already there. Position the volumetric flask at the end of the condenser and put the stoppers in place on alcohol apparatus Erlenmeyer flask and condenser. Turn the cold water on through the condenser of the apparatus and turn on heat source. When the alcohol distillate reaches ¾ inch below the neck of the volumetric flask, turn both heat and water off. Remove stoppers. Add distilled water to bring the contents of volumetric flask up to the blue line and mix well. Then place this flask into refrigerator until cooled to 60° F.

Pour the contents of the volumetric flask into the hydrometer jar and put the Tralle hydrometer in the cylinder. A direct reading of this hydrometer will give you the percentage alcohol by volume. The results are usually reported to the nearest 0.1 percent.

Ebullioscope method. This is the method most generally used for dry dinner wines in commercial wineries and is based on the regular variation in the boiling point of mixtures of water and alcohol. While there are several different types of ebullioscopes on

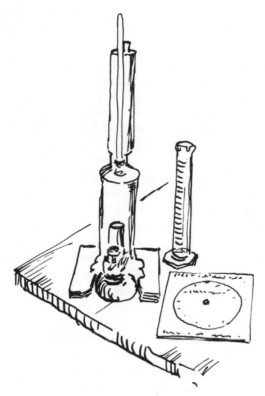

Fig. 22: The equipment arrangement used in the distillation (left) and ebullioscope (right) methods for determining alcoholic percentage.

the market, most consist of a small boiling chamber, a standard thermometer—the bulb of which is inserted into the boiling chamber—a metal reflux condenser, a small ethyl alcohol lamp, a measuring cylinder, and a special circular slide rule that has a special adjustable scale indicating the relation between boiling point and alcohol of the sample. The ebullioscope is used as follows:

Rinse the ebullioscope thoroughly with distilled water. Fill the front tube (the boiling chamber) with fifty milliliters of distilled water. Put the thermometer in the front opening of the ebullioscope. Place the lighted alcohol burner under the front tube and bring the water to the boiling point. (The boiling point is determined when the mercury of the thermometer remains constant.)

Using the circular slide rule, record the reading of the boiling point of water and set the dial with the degree of boiling water at zero.

After the boiling point of water is determined empty the contents of the ebullioscope. Rinse the center and front tubes of the device with a wine sample and then place fifty milliliters of the wine sample in the front tube. Place water in outer cylinder around the center tube (the condenser) and bring wine to a boil as was done for the water. Once the boiling point of the wine is known, read the degrees on the center dial of the slide rule (do not turn the dial) and the corresponding figure will tell the alcohol content of the wine in percentage by volume. Results of this method are reported only to the nearest 0.1 percent.

The simplest and quickest way of ascertaining the quantity of alcohol in a wine, and one used by most home winemakers, is with a vinometer (see page 25), but while reasonably accurate for most tasks, it is not comparable in total accuracy with the distillation procedure or ebullioscope method. Regardless of the method of testing, the wine's alcoholic content will generally be found to range from 11 to 13 percent by volume when it has been properly fermented. Should the test prove that the alcoholic content is deficient, but the wine is dry of sugar, it would be a good idea to blend it with a wine of a higher alcoholic percentage. If sugar remains, check the sulfur dioxide content and aerate if over 20 ppm free. If not, try to ferment out the remaining sugar by following the same technique as for a stuck fermentation (see page 73).

Testing for Acidity. The acidity of a finished wine is due to some extent both to so-called fixed acids and to volatile acids. The latter are products of fermentation, while the fixed acids—tartaric and malic—are those found naturally in the grapes. Without the volatile acids—carbonic, propionic, butyric, and acetic acids— wine would develop little true bouquet. But their presence in more than a very small amount is invariably a sign of problems ahead for the winemaker.

The first step in testing for volatile acidity is to determine the total acidity by following the same procedure that is employed in determining the total acidity of the must before fermentation (see page 65). These pre-fermentation acids, of course, are of the fixed variety and should reduce considerably during fermentation.

As a matter of fact, if the total acidity of the new wine is lower than was the total acidity of the must, and should it have a clean, vinous smell, it is then fairly safe to assume that the wine is sound and it is not necessary to determine what proportion of the total consists of fixed acids and what is volatile acids.

On the other hand, should the total acidity of the new wine be equal to or higher than that of the must from which it was made, then the winemaker should conduct a test to find out whether the volatile acidity exceeds the safe minimum. The first of these is conducted by using your nose. Since the undesirable volatile acids have very pungent odors, they can generally be easily detected before they reach the danger point. Propionic and acetic acids have the characteristic odor of vinegar, while butyric acid smells much like rancid butter.

A more exacting method, of course, is by chemical test involving a suitable volatile acid still. Such a still is shown in Fig. 23 and consists of an outer round-bottom 1,000-ml wide-mouthed boiling flask, an inner cylindrical tube fitted inside the boiling flask through a wide stopper and connected to a vertically set Liebig condenser. Also have on hand a 10-ml pipette, 10/N sodium hydroxide solution, 1 percent phenolphthalein solution, a buret stand, distilled water, heat source for the boiling flask, a cold-water connection, and a drain for the condenser. The test is conducted as follows:

Start the cold water flowing through the condenser. Then fill the boiling flask approximately three-quarters full and remove the clamp from the short rubber tubing at the side of the flask. Heat the water to boiling for two or three minutes. Reduce the heat. Place a 250-ml Erlenmeyer flask under the outlet of the condenser. Previously mark the 100-milliliter level on this flask. Introduce 10 milliliters of wine by pipette into the inner tube. Insert the stopper connecting it to the condenser. Increase the heat and bring the water to boiling; when it is boiling vigorously replace the clamp, thus closing the rubber tubing at the side of the flask. Continue boiling until 100 ml of liquid distills over into the 250-ml flask. Open the clamp on the side piece of rubber tubing so that the wine will not suck back into the boiling flask and turn off the flame.

To the distillate in the Erlenmeyer flask add several drops of the phenolphthalein solution and titrate with sodium hydroxide solu-

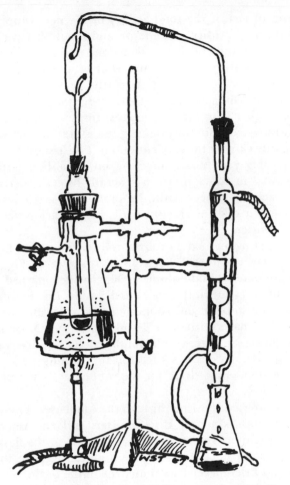

Fig. 23: The arrangement of a volatile acid still.

tion in the same manner as for the total acids test until it turns pink. Then take the number of milliliters used of sodium hydroxide solution and multiply it by 0.015. The result will give you the amount of volatile acid present. For example, if 3 ml of sodium hydroxide are used the grams of volatile acidity per 100 ml equals 3.0 × 0.015 or 0.045 grams.

Sound new wines should show less than 0.05 grams of volatile acidity per 100 ml and a sound aged wine less than 0.08. (The present United States Government legal maximum limits of volatile acidity are 0.12 grams per 100 ml for white wines and 0.14 grams for red wines, exclusive of sulfur dioxide.) An appreciable rise in the volatile acidity in a wine during storage indicates bacterial spoilage, and it should be finished as rapidly as possible. This means it should be racked immediately from its lees, and dosed with sodium or potassium metabisulfite at a rate of 80 to 100 ppm. The wine then should be fined, chilled, and inspected frequently.

If the volatile acidity is already to the point at which the wine has a very disagreeable smell, the only wise thing to do is throw it away immediately since a badly sick wine can never be brought back to good health. It is foolish to try to save a bad wine by blending it with a good one. The only thing you will have is a double batch of bad wine.

Should the wine be sound and good-smelling, but have a high total acidity, it can be blended with a low-acid wine and results may be most favorable. Likewise, a wine with a low total acidity may be successful blended with a high-acid one.

Blending Wines. Blending has often been called "the advanced stage of the winemaker's craft." While it is true that experience and training, plus a keen sense of smell and of taste, play an important part in the blending of wines, it is a skill that home winemakers will have to learn if they wish to produce palatable wines year in and year out. Actually, a great deal of fun can be had by blending wines to your taste and often you can come up with an excellent wine. Within the limits of this general objective there are certain specific objectives you can try to accomplish: A weak wine can be made healthier and stronger by blending it with one of high alcoholic content; acidity can be decreased or increased through blending with another wine of appropriate contrasting qualities; the vinosity of poorer wines can be improved; the harshness of new wines can be smoothed out by blending with an older, more matured wine; the color of a wine often can be heightened by blending; and a wine can be created with a "new" taste.

There are really no hard-and-fast rules of blending. For instance, wines may be blended after fermentation or at any other point in the finishing process. Generally, however, it is best for the beginner to wait for the wine to mature and see what it makes of itself. If, when it should be ready for bottling, you do not like it for some characteristic reason, then put it aside until you have another to blend with it. It is not wise to hurry matters when blending; no advantage is lost by waiting.

Normally, the wines that are blended together should be of the same approximate age, except when it is desired to reduce the "greenness" of a young wine. But, when this is done, be sure to add a fully-aged wine from the same or a similar grape. Also, a wine that has overaged can be made more drinkable and fresh by adding to it a strong young wine of the same sort.

Even though all the components of the wine blend may have been brilliantly clear before mixing, either a clouding or a precipitation will often occur after blending. Sometimes this change is due to the actual precipitation of tartrates or the formation of metal cloudiness (casse); at other times it results from over-aeration and is cured by standing. If the wine should not remain clear, it may have to be refined or otherwise treated as described later in this chapter.

The juice of some grapes is ideal for blending, while others tend to "overpower" desirable tastes. The Concord grape juice, for example, when used in excess of 5 percent of the total amount, tends to give the finished wine more or less a "Concord taste." More information on the blending characteristics of grapes is given in Chapter Three.

In making blending tests, the winemaker should have the desired result clearly in mind. Haphazard blending is of little value and may do considerable damage to wines of desirable characteristic flavors. To avoid risking large quantities of wine, it is wise to first make a small blend in a graduated glass or flask. When your taste tells you that everything is fine, then make the large blend proportionately. If, for example, it requires 20 ml of wine A and 30 ml of wine B to produce a very palatable mixture then this means that the wine should be blended in the proportion of 2 to 3, or 1 to $1\frac{1}{2}$. There is no limit to how many portions you can mix together until you feel that you have found the perfect balance. But the final blend should always be stored for several weeks before bottling.

While blending is a great advantage to the winemaker, it is not a cure-all for his problems. Bad wines, even in small amounts, may contaminate or dilute good ones, and the good wine will thus depreciate in value. That is, never blend a sound wine with an unsound one. The basic suggestions on blending hold good for both red and white wines.

Racking and Fining. The first racking for red wines should be done in mid-December. Rack it again in February and again just before hot weather—May or June. It should be racked a fourth time in October, in order to rid it of any sediment that may have been thrown down during the hot weather. If the wine is to be held longer before bottling, rack it once or twice a year. But between rackings the container should be kept completely filled to avoid spoilage. A wooden container generally requires additional wine about twice a month; a glass one does not need the addition of new wine quite so frequently. The sulfur dioxide level should be kept at twenty to thirty parts per million at all times.

The actual racking for red wines is carried on in the same manner as for the white types. Make certain that the siphoning hose has been soaked in water heated to just below the boiling point, and the container that is to receive the racked wine is thoroughly cleaned and rinsed. Once a container has been emptied, rinse it several times and it should then be ready to receive the racked wine from the next container.

Sparkolloid and bentonite may be employed as fining agents for red wines and are used as described on page 79. Many old-time winemakers prefer to use gelatin in fining red wines. The gelatin forms a coarse flocculation by combining with some of the tannin that is present in good amounts in red wine. The wine's suspended matter is entrained by the flocculating material and drawn to the bottom as the finings gradually settle. The gelatin—about 2 grams per 5 gallons of wine—is dissolved in a small quantity of warm water, added to the wine, and stirred in. (Unflavored household gelatin may be used for this purpose.) Gelatin fining is most effective on warm wine and normally takes from two to five days to clear the wine. When gelatin fining is used with white wines, powdered tannin should be added beforehand in a dose equal in weight to the amount of gelatin added.

Regardless of the fining agents used, the operation should be undertaken before the wine has achieved stability. This usually means from mid-January to mid-March, if it is kept in very cool cellars. But, once the finings have fallen to the bottom of the container and the wine is bright, be sure to rack it as soon as possible since long contact with these agents can sometimes cause off-flavors. Stabilize in a refrigerator as with the white wine.

Filtration. This procedure, as distinct from fining, is an entirely physical operation. By definition, a liquid filtration consists in the removal of solid particles in suspension for the purpose of improving the appearance of the filtrate. While the theory of filtration is very simple, in practice considerable ingenuity has been displayed by the inventors of the various types of filters which are known to the wine trade, the original idea of a strainer being worked upon in connection with such forces as molecular attraction and adhesion. This has led to the employment of specially prepared linen, paper, porcelain, etc., and in the operation of filtration, as the minute particles in the wine deposit upon the sides or surface of the filter, they tend by their own means to render the filtration more perfect. Basically, the two filtration techniques within the reach of the home winemaker employ asbestos pulp and filter paper.

In the latter method, it is preferable to use two filter papers of different degrees of fineness. These papers are placed together, the coarser one on top so that it will be inside; the papers are then folded in half and then in half again to make a quarter. The flaps are then folded back onto the fold, then once more back on themselves so that these portions are a sixteenth of the whole while the center piece is an eighth. Holding the folded flaps, open the paper to the original quarter and fold the flaps inward toward the inside of the fold. The cone is then bent back at the original quarter fold so as to bring the fold outward. The folded papers are then opened out and a perfect fluted filter cone is the result. The cone is then placed on a small cushion of sterile cotton inside the stainless steel funnel. This helps to protect the point and prevents it from breaking. During the folding, care must be taken not to press the folds down to the point, as that would put an undue strain on the paper. The whole purpose of fluting the paper is to present a larger filtration surface, which will tend to speed up the output. The wine to be filtered is poured into the cone. The filter papers are available from the suppliers listed in Appendix C.

With the asbestos pulp technique, a handful of pulp for about five gallons—less for a gallon—is mixed into wine while it is still in the container. (Asbestos pulp is available from many wine supply dealers.) Then take a stainless steel funnel, which has been loosely plugged with some sterile cotton, rest the weight of a stainless steel tablespoon on this cotton to hold the plug down, pour the asbestos-wine mixture on this and return the first filtrate back to the funnel until the filtrate runs clear. Do not remove the spoon from the funnel or let the asbestos drain dry but keep on topping up the liquid in the funnel with the cloudy wine. This method of clarifying is quicker than filtration through filter paper. Actually, both methods are slow, but they can be speeded up when done in conjunction with a filter pump shown in Fig. 24. The tap on the running water draws out the air from the conical flask and creates a partial vacuum in it. As nature abhors a vacuum the wine is sucked through the filter paper or asbestos pulp into the flask at a faster rate than gravity alone could provide.

In addition to the fact that both techniques are slow and not suitable for large volumes of wine, they create a situation in which the wine has far too much chance to oxidize and give up its flavor to the surrounding air. While many commercial wineries today use speedy filtration, equipment for this is very expensive and the average home seldom has the chance to use such filtration arrangements, unless they can be rented from a wine supplier. If you live near some of the supply firms listed in Appendix C, it is possible that they may have suitable filtration equipment at low rental rates. But otherwise the home winemaker is best advised to follow a course of simple clarification, which, of course, is the fining method that has been previously described.

Bottling. Red wines are rarely bottled as early as white wines. It is good to wait until they are *at least* one year old; some are much better after two, three, or four years of aging in the container. This is especially true when the aging is done in good oak cooperage, since it does undoubtedly contribute subtly to the development of the flavor and bouquet. The smaller the oak container, the greater the aging—40- to 50-gallon barrels age more slowly than 10- or 15-gallon ones. Remember that too much aging can be worse than too little. It is up to your good judgment and *taste* to decide.

The bottling operation is carried on in the same manner as for white wine. In general, bottle aging has a more marked effect on red wines than on white ones. Some relatively ordinary red wines undergo a great improvement when permitted to age for two, five, or even ten years in the bottle. But most red wines reach their maximum of quality after a year or two in the bottle.

RED WINE SUMMARY

The major difference between red and white winemaking, aside from the varieties of grapes used, occurs right at the beginning of the vintage. The grapes are crushed as in the white wine process, but then collected and fermented in a crock or tub. These grapes are then placed in an open-end vat and are allowed to ferment for five to ten days; the "cap" which rises to the top is pushed down into the liquid two or three times a day. The grapes are then pressed—it is now considerably easier—and we proceed exactly as with white wines. It is generally felt that the reds should ferment a little more rapidly and at higher temperatures than the whites. They also require more maturing before being ready to drink.

DRY WINES

By and large, most quality red and white wines are dry, and for most people a dry taste has to be acquired, since we are accustomed in the United States to a sweet taste, which is not natural in most wines. When one acquires a taste for dry, quality wines, his enjoyment of wine increases manyfold and he will be able to appreciate the true character and flavor of the individual wine grapes. Some dry wines, labeled as such, are really not dry red or white wines, as they contain amounts of fermentable or residual sugar. The following table gives approximate figures for extract, acidity, and Balling of quality dry red and dry white wine.

	RED	WHITE
Alcohol by volume	12%	12%
Balling	$-1.7°$ per ml	$-2.0°$ per ml
Extract	2.2	+1.8
Total acidity	0.600 to 0.700	0.550 to 0.650
Volatile acidity	0.03 to 0.07	0.025 to 0.065

NOTE: *Terms above, except alcohol and Balling, are expressed in grams per 100 milliliters.*

MAKING PINK, OR ROSÉ, WINE

There are three basic ways to make pink, or rosé, wine. The easiest and best way for the home winemaker to produce such a product is to blend together a good white wine and a good red wine. When making a pink wine in this manner, follow the basic rules of blending given earlier in this chapter.

The second procedure for making a pink wine is simply a partial fermenting of red grapes on the skins (about eighteen to thirty-six hours); while they are still fermenting, press them so that not all the color is taken from the skins. Visual observation will indicate when the must has acquired the desired pink color.

Still another method of making pink wine is to follow the red wine procedure exactly, but select a variety of grape that is suitable for rosé wines, one that has only a small amount of color in its skins. Such grapes as Seibel 1000, Steuben, and Isabella can be fermented all the way on the skins and still only have a light red or pink color.

While pink wines may follow the same fermentation procedure as for red wines, they need the care and precautions of the white types. That is, they must be stored in a cool location (between 50° and 60° F.) and care must be taken to prevent oxidation, which will cause a pink wine to turn orange or brown. This also produces off-flavors as well as the undesirable color characteristics. Pink wines unlike red or white ones should be drunk as quickly as possible after they are bottle clear and have been racked a couple of times. We would suggest that the home winemaker follow a rule of thumb that pink wines should be fresh wines— never kept for more than a year.

PERILS AND PITFALLS

Winemaking, as we have stated earlier, is not yet a science, it is an art—an art which is dependent on the maker's skill, good judgment and good fortune. There are times when one, if not all three, of these important requirements will be missing and the result will be poor wine. The upcoming information may be a sad ending for a happy chapter, but is very necessary.

Acetification. The first and foremost peril of home winemaking is acetification, or vinegar formation. Vinegar bacteria are found in overripe or damaged grapes and are introduced by the tiny flies (*Drosophila* species) which are always found hovering around decaying fruit or spilled wine. The bacteria thrive under certain conditions. First of all they require air or oxygen and a weak alcohol solution, which they convert into vinegar. By keeping your winery and its equipment clean, by employing only sound, ripe grapes, by using sulfur dioxide, by fermenting to a sufficiently high alcohol strength, and by keeping containers full once the primary fermentation is over, vinegar formation can be prevented. There is no remedy once much vinegar is present. By tasting your wine at frequent intervals you can prevent excessive acetification. At the slightest sign of vinegar formation the wine must be treated.

If much vinegar has formed the only thing to do is to throw it away or let the wine turn completely and, when it has finished its transformation, bottle it, and pasteurize the bottles to preserve the vinegar. Pasteurizing is carried out by placing the bottles upright with loosened caps in a large cooking utensil. Fill with warm water out of the tap and heat slowly to 175° F. Remove the cooking utensil from the stove and leave the bottles in the water for another ten minutes. Then tighten the caps, pour off the water, remove the bottles and allow them to cool back to room temperature. Some clouding may result from the heat required for pasteurization but it is harmless and will form sediment if the bottles are left undisturbed. Actually, if the bottles are stored at 40° to 50° F. for a week or two, they will partially clarify themselves by depositing suspended material. When ready for use, the clear vinegar above the sediment should be decanted off into another bottle.

Wine vinegar is much appreciated by the gourmet. Also, using the wine vinegar as a base, many types of flavored vinegars may be prepared. Remove a small amount of vinegar from a bottle and add the flavoring material desired. Then refill the bottle. In a week or two, the vinegar will assume the flavor of the added material, and may then be used. The most popular flavoring materials are tarragon, chives, dill, garlic, orégano, and onion powder. Mixtures of certain herbs may also be employed.

Any of the winery equipment that came in contact with the

acetified wine should be thoroughly sterilized to kill the vinegar bacteria. Incidentally, *never* make vinegar in your wine cellar or purposely use any of your winemaking equipment for vinegar production. The tremendous numbers of bacteria involved never make it a safe winery operation.

Flowers of Wine. This peril is recognized as small whitish particles, or "flowers," on the surface of the wine. Unless attended to, these multiply rapidly until the whole surface is covered by a thick bacterial film and wine will be ruined. Since this disease is due to a yeastlike body called *mycoderma,* the wine should be given a dose of sulfur dioxide as soon as the flecks appear and then racked off into clean nonwooden containers, which must be filled to the top. Since these flowers can only develop in the presence of air, make sure that wine, once rid of the plague, has no surface contact with air, by keeping the container filled and tightly sealed.

Lactic Acid Haze. A silky sheen that may be seen on rare occasions when the wine is swirled. To correct this pitfall, raise the sulfur dioxide level of the wine to at least 80 ppm. In a few days, the wine should then be fined or filtered.

Pectin Haze. One of the common causes of persistent cloudiness or haze in home-made wine is pectin. This exists in practically all fruit and is, of course, the element which makes jelly and jam possible. There is also an enzyme in grapes which tends to break down pectin but it is not always present in sufficient quantities. If these pectins are not broken down, they will persist in the wine in the form of a haze. Accordingly, you will be wise to add pectic enzymes, which can be purchased under various trade names, to the fresh must or juice, or even to the wine itself.

Metal Casse. The wine develops a white or colored haze which is due to metallic contaminations, such as traces of aluminum, zinc, iron, or copper. The addition of some citric acid will generally remove some of the discoloration due to copper or iron. The best way to avoid this pitfall is to use only glass, plastic, stoneware, wood and stainless steel items in your winery.

Overoxidation. Too much air space in the storage container, failure to keep the fermentation lock filled with water, and overhandling (filtering, fining, or racking too often) leads to the common fault of overoxidation. As the term implies, this means simply that the wine has gotten too much oxygen. This leads to a darkening of the wine, which, by itself is bearable; but, as we have stressed so many times, it also leads to an off-taste which is sometimes described as cooked and is often reminiscent of a spoiled sherry.

Overacidity. Sometimes the new wine is too high in acid. One of the best ways to help the wine along is to increase the stabilization period (see page 80). Of course, you can mask the flavor by adding a little sugar, but be sure to raise the SO_2 level to 60 to 80 ppm. When the grapes have a very high acid content, you may overcome this to some degree by stirring in a paste of 2 grams of calcium carbonate (chalk) per gallon of must. It will foam up, so give it room. The chalk will precipitate. You may also follow the techniques described on pages 65 and 97.

Medicinal or Bitter Taste. This is due mainly to unsuitable yeast and lack of acidity during the fermentation. It often can occur in red wines owing to moldy grapes. It must be avoided as there is little cure for it; with crossed fingers you can try adding a little citric acid.

A "mousy" taste can be cured by adding one gram of potassium or sodium metabisulfite to the gallon of wine and by stirring vigorously. The wine should then be filtered or fined. The cause of this is often residual sugar and it does not often occur in strong dry wines.

A "musty" flavor is caused by not racking soon enough. It is best to throw away any wine with this flavor.

Flat Taste. This is caused by a lack of astringent matter, notably tannin. Add a small amount of tannic acid (see page 36).

Sour or Astringent Taste. (Not to be confused with an overacid taste). It is usually caused by undesirable yeasts and bacteria or storage in a wooden container that is too new. An *attempt* can be made to correct this problem by stirring ten grams of activated carbon into every ten gallons of wine (see page 37). Let stand for three or four days and then rack into a fresh container. A gelatin fining may also help. If carbon is used you must have a filter.

Mysterious Tastes. Moldy tastes, odor of fuel or kerosene, the taste of wood or cork, and other uncharacteristic flavors are generally caused by carelessness of the winemaker—the use of unclean equipment, of excessively moldy fruit, of improperly prepared cooperage, or by the exposure of wine to strong odors such as that of gasoline.

Decoloring Wine. Despite all efforts, sometimes it is possible, when using dark grapes for white wines, to get some pigment from the skins in the juice. While this added color will not generally affect the taste, you may wish to decolor the wine to make it white in appearance. This can be done, after the second racking, by adding some activated carbon (charcoal) to the wine in the proportion of 5 grams to every 5 gallons. The carbon is first stirred into a little wine drawn from the container and then is thoroughly mixed with the whole. The carbon has the property of absorbing coloring matter, but the wine must be clarified by filtering.

Chapter Six

Making Champagne and
Sparkling Wines

The beginning home winemaker may have some qualms about his ability to produce sparkling wines such as champagne. While it might not be advisable for him to start right off with them the first year, after that there is nothing about its making that should prove too difficult. As a matter of fact there are home winemakers producing it all over the country, and many are doing a very fine job too. The cost of making it yourself compared to buying it is so low that you can easily afford to develop a "champagne thirst."

PREPARATION OF THE WINE

In the spring when it is possible to judge accurately last fall's wines, select a good, sound white dinner wine for use in your champagne making. We emphasize the words *good* and *sound* since it is the height of folly to spend the considerable amount of time and effort involved in champagne making on a wine of doubtful quality. The wine should be thoroughly clarified and stabilized. It should be no more than a light straw, or low yellow, in color and be light in body, with alcoholic volume content between 10 and 11 percent. (A wine of more than 11 percent may not properly referment.) The "bite" which we all enjoy and expect from the bubbles of fine champagne will be increased if the wine has sufficient acidity, about 0.7 percent. The wine should also contain tannin, partly to obtain good clarification before refermentation and partly to guard against cloudiness after refermentation. Thus the wine that is to be rendered sparkling should receive, if necessary, a dose of tannic acid early in its life (see pages 36 and 79). The alcoholic percentage, total acidity, and sugar content tests that were fully described in Chapters 4 and 5 will confirm these facts about the white wine you propose to use.

Avoid also a wine that has a residue of fermentable sugar. Since the quantitative chemical test for residual sugar is generally too complicated for the home winemaker, you can only rely on the diabetic tape test (see page 72). If the wine is perceptibly sweet, do not employ it for champagne making.

If no single wine meets these requirements it may be advisable to blend. In the East, Delaware and Catawba are a common and excellent base for blending. A blend that we have found superior is 50 percent Delaware, 35 percent Seyval Blanc, and 15 percent Catawba. Other grapes with high potential for these wines are Dutchess, Aurora, White Riesling, and of course the classic champagne varieties: Pinot Blanc, Pinot Noir, and Pinot Chardonnay. Because of their acidity and tannin content, however, eastern grapes are considered to make the best possible sparkling wines.

The wine, whether blended or not, is siphoned or racked into a suitable fermenter, or storage container. (A clean 5-gallon glass carboy or jug is ideal.) Check the sugar content with a −0.5 to +0.5 Balling hydrometer. Then add sugar until the hydrometer reads +0.5. Do not exceed this amount and measure very carefully. If considerably more sugar is added than 0.5 Balling it may "blow up" the bottles as the sparkling wine is fermenting. If less sugar is added, it will not create sufficient carbon dioxide with which to finish the wine later. The sugar should be added as a syrup, which is prepared by dissolving cane sugar in a suitable quantity of wine. The syrup is poured into the wine and the container shaken thoroughly. Be sure to shake it several times so that the sugar dissolves completely.

After the sugar has been added and is well dissolved, the sulfur dioxide should be checked and it should be adjusted to below 15 ppm free. If the sulfur dioxide is over this level, it may inhibit the yeast cells and you will have a stuck fermentation in the bottles. Also at this point, a yeast nutrient should be added. Most yeast nutrients are comprised of ammonium phosphate or ammonium sulfate, and this gives the yeast cells a new nitrogen source to replace the one that was used up—or mostly so—in the first fermentation of the wine. In addition, most yeast nutrients contain B vitamins and other necessary constituents for the building of healthy yeast cells. The nutrient is usually added in amounts of approximately 5 to 10 grams per 10 gallons of cuvée. (A still wine that is made or blended for the explicit purpose of being made into champagne is known as a *cuvée wine*.) Sometimes there are enough yeast cells still present in the new wine, even though it has been racked two or three times, to start the second fermentation. After a good clarification, however, most viable yeast cells have been removed.

Many home winemakers, because of previous failures to referment the wine with existing cells—many of these failures occurred *before* the common use of yeast nutrients—inoculate their cuvée with a vigorous champagne strain of yeast. The liquid yeast starter is prepared and introduced into the cuvée container in the same manner as described on page 70, except for the use of a small amount of the cuvée wine sweetened to about $+20°$ Balling as a growing medium instead of grape juice.

BOTTLE FERMENTATION

When fermentation has definitely begun—usually within twenty-four to thirty-six hours—siphon the wine into $\frac{1}{10}$ or $\frac{1}{5}$ gallon champagne bottles; fill to about $1\frac{1}{2}$ inches from the top. As each bottle is filled, it should be temporarily capped immediately with a crown (beer bottle type) cap. (A special crown capper device is required to apply these caps.) Be sure to use only *sound* cham-

Fig. 24: A simple clearing rack.

pagne bottles. These are specially made to withstand high pressures; a first-quality *new* champagne bottle is designed to withstand a pressure of better than two hundred pounds per square inch, but it is never called on to do so. Second-hand champagne bottles cannot stand as great pressures as new ones. The bottles, of course, should be washed and rinsed thoroughly. Actually, they should be washed again shortly before they are to be filled.

While bottling, make sure that the yeast cells remain in suspension in the cuvée batch container. In order to keep these cells from precipitating to the bottom of the container, it is a good idea, after every six or eight bottles are filled, to stir the cuvée *gently*, with a clean glass rod, to keep the yeast in suspension. Lay the bottles on their sides in the wine cellar; temperature may range from 55° to 70° F.; however, it should be kept as constant as possible. The most orderly fashion to store the bottles is to use the tierage system shown in Fig. 26. It is wise during the bottling, capping, and tierage processes to have the assistance of your wife or one of your winemaking buddies. It will save time and get the cuvée in the bottles without any chance to spoil.

RIDDLING, DISGORGING, AND THE DOSAGE

As the wine ferments the yeast will slowly precipitate as sediment down to the bottom of the bottle, leaving a clear wine above.

This secondary or bottle fermentation will take anywhere from one to three weeks to complete. The variation in the time factor depends upon the variety of wine that is in the bottle, the yeast that is employed, the temperature of the cellar, etc. All precautions should be used to avoid injury from the possible breaking of a bottle under pressure. While the new champagne bottles provide a wide margin of safety and seldom explode under the pressure built up inside, we strongly advise the home winemaker to wear a face shield and a pair of stout gloves.

The bottles should remain in tierage for at least one year—two years is even better. During this ripening period, it is believed that as the yeast sporate and die their cell walls crack and allow some of the protoplasm inside the yeast cell to become dissolved with the wine, giving it a yeasty or champagne-type flavor.

To remove the sediment (the spent yeast cells), the ancient process known as *riddling* is used. The bottles are removed from tierage and placed in a special rack constructed so that the bottles can be stored neck down at an angle of about 70° during the riddling process. A simple clearing rack is shown in Fig. 24.

Riddling is performed by raising the bottle from the rack, turning a quarter turn clockwise, and dropping it with a gentle thump back into its resting place. This gentle jarring action starts the sediment sliding along the inside walls of the bottle down toward the neck. The bottles should be riddled twice a day for about three weeks or until candling under a strong light shows that all the sediment is in the neck of the bottles.

When the riddling is completed, sediment in the neck of the bottle is removed by the disgorging process. As the name implies, the sediment, after the temporary cap is removed, is discharged with considerable force from the bottle. When you are ready to disgorge the sediment, the bottles should be placed outdoors or in some other cool location for a final chilling. At this lowered temperature the carbon dioxide gas in the wine remains more soluble, thus less pressure will be lost during the disgorging. During the chilling operation, the bottles should, of course, stay neck down in a soft-drink case or in baskets.

When the bottles are chilled (40° F is an ideal temperature), a brine of coarse salt and chipped ice should be prepared and placed in a washtub. Then the chilled bottles are inserted, still neck

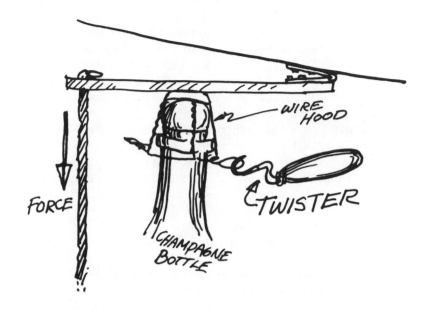

Fig. 25: Method of installing the wire hood.

down, into the brine solution, to a depth of 1 to 1½ inches. In this solution, the wine, including the sediment deposited there, will freeze into a solid plug of ice. It will take anywhere from one-half to one hour for this freezing of the plug to take place.

Once the plug is frozen, take the bottle from the brine and dip the neck in a pan of warm water. This will rinse the brine from around the bottle neck and will help to slightly loosen the ice plug. Then, holding the bottle upward at a 45° angle, remove the cap with a bottle-cap opener, and let the plug blow out.

After the plug has blown out, put your thumb over the opening and very gently set the bottle down on a table. Quickly, but gently, pour into the bottle a dosage of about 25 ml of brandy in which 10 grams of cane sugar have been dissolved—among other things this sugar, being already dissolved, will tend to quiet the wine. Also, with the amount of carbon dioxide present in sparkling wines, they will be very astringent and bitter unless they are sweetened a little. Our preference is 10 grams of sugar in a fifth-size bottle. We also suggest that you prepare your dosage in bulk to cover all the bottles you plan to disgorge at any one time. Add sodium or potassium metabisulfite to a level of 800 ppm in your dosage solution. A typical solution for 25 to 30 one-fifth bottles is as follows: ⅕ gallon of brandy = 757 ml; cane sugar = 220 grams; metabisulfite = 2½ grams. If you prefer a sweeter champagne, increase the sugar dosage to your taste.

Once the dosage has been gently poured into the bottle, the next step is to cork it. While many home winemakers like to use new plastic champagne corks because they need not be soaked, they are simple to drive into a bottle, and they are easy to get a wire hood around, we still prefer the natural wood champagne corks. The plastic corks do not allow the champagne to continue aging, and we have, through experimentation, found adverse tastes from plastic after a short period of time.

To install the wire hood, which holds either type of cork in place, the loop of wire is passed over the neck of the bottle; the two ends are brought up over the cork and separated to give two separate holdings, then down the other side, under the wire, pulled

Fig. 26: Storage bin suggestions for the home winery.

hard, twisted together and pressed up flat to the bottle. The wire hoods and a tool to make their installation easy are available from any of the suppliers listed in Appendix C.

When all the bottles have been corked and the wire hoods installed, lay the bottles back into tierage to rest on their sides for a period of not less than two months. During this time, inspect the bottles occasionally to make certain that the corks are not leaking. A leaker can be identified by a dark syrupy solution oozing out between the top lip of the bottle just underneath where the cork is fitted.

OTHER SPARKLING WINES

A very dry champagne, or one whose dosage has very little sugar, is generally called *brut*. (Our 10-gram sugar dosage is considered a brut champagne.) A sweet champagne might be called *dry*, while a very sweet one, (comparable to those of Spumante in Italy, might be referred to as *doux*. Most home winemakers who are very proud of their cuvée wine usually make their champagne as brut as they can. Of course, sugar is a very fine masker, and should something happen along the way in the preparation of the still wine or the cuvée a lot can be covered up by the addition of higher amounts of sugar.

In this chapter we have discussed only the traditional method of making champagne. This method has long been considered the only true one by most good winemakers and is the method many wineries in both France and the United States employ to produce premium-quality champagne. A few large commercial wineries in the western part of our country produce sparkling wines by the bulk or Charmat process. In this method, the secondary fermentation and clearing processes take place in closed stainless steel tanks. The finished wine is transferred from these tanks to the bottles under pressure. This method becomes a little expensive and difficult for the home winemaker, and it does not usually turn out premium-quality champagne. We would also recommend that the home winemaker *not* undertake to make carbonated wines because of the equipment that is needed to perform the task correctly. In addition, these wines cannot be considered on the same level as high-quality, bottle-fermented champagne. The yeasty taste does not come through in a carbonated wine and it is generally considered that a carbonated wine is inferior to champagne.

All our references to this point have been to a cuvée of white wines. Red wines can be made sparkling by following the same traditional French or bottle fermentation method, and are called "red champagne," "sparkling Burgundy," or "champagne rouge." When rosé or pink wines are given the same process they are called "sparkling rosé," or "pink champagne." It takes a little more time to produce sparkling wines than still ones, but it will seem time well spent when you taste the results of your labors.

Chapter Seven

Making Dessert Wines

The sweet, full-bodied wines served with desserts and as refreshments in the afternoon or evening are called *dessert wines*. They range from medium sweet to very sweet, and in color from pale gold to deep red. Their alcoholic content generally ranges from about 17 to 22 percent.

Since it is difficult to get natural fermentation, as described in the earlier chapters of this book, much above 14 percent, most dessert wines are fortified with an outside source of alcohol, generally brandy, to raise their alcoholic content. Some home winemakers *approximate* dessert wine by a method of syruped fermentation. The fermentation is started as if a dry table wine were to be produced. When the fermentation is very active and the hydrometer reads about 5° Balling, sugar or grape concentrate is added to raise the reading to 10°. The fermentation will be activated, particularly when concentrate is used. When the reading again reaches 5°, add more sugar or concentrate. Three or four additions may be necessary. By this method an alcohol content of 16 or 17 percent will be attained under favorable conditions with only top-grade high-alcohol-producing yeast strains.

These wines are *not* very stable and much care and attention must be given them to prevent bacterial growth. The wine should be stored in a cool place, and must be frequently racked in order to separate it from the yeast and other microorganisms. Filtration is very desirable. About 1/4 ounce of potassium metabisulfite should be added to each 10 gallons of wine upon completion of fermentation. Such wines should not be bottled until they are stable and show no signs of refermentation. Even then it is wise to store the bottles in an upright position so that if the wines start to referment the corks will blow out rather than having the bottle break. One or two years' aging in wooden containers can be helpful to the flavor.

FORTIFIED WINES

A much surer (and safer) method of making dessert wines is to fortify them. As we already know, fortified wines are wines to which alcohol has been added. This is done to sweet wines because the increase in alcoholic content stops all fermentation and prevents it from recurring again. Most wines are fortified up to a minimum of 18 percent and a usual maximum of 22 percent of alcohol. The two major types of fortified wines are sherry and port.

In general, we do not recommend that the home winemaker endeavor to make fortified wines. While in our lifetime we have tasted a number of good sherries and ports produced by home winemakers, the major reason for our opposition is that tax-paid beverage brandy makes the cost of such wines too high. The brandy also contributes its own flavor and taste to the wine rather than just raising its alcohol content. Commercial wineries get around this by purchasing in vast amounts 190-proof brandy which is nearly odorless and tasteless to add to their dessert wines. This type of brandy is next to impossible for the home winemaker to obtain in bond (tax unpaid).

Sherry. The first step in the making of sherry is to determine what still wine the brandy should be added to. If you wish a dark sherry, pick a relatively dark red wine. When a pale dry sherry is desired, select a white wine. In any case, whatever wine you choose to fortify, it should *not* be one of your best, at least for a first try.

Before taking a look at the actual sherry-making techniques, let us first discuss the two ways in which alcohol content of beverages are measured—percentage and degree of proof. Percentage, as has been previously stated, is determined by volume—12 percent wine would contain 12 parts alcohol and 88 parts water, acids, glycerols, etc. Proof degrees are defined in the United States as spirits containing, in 100 volumes, 50 volumes of absolute alcohol of specific gravity 0.7939 and 53.71 volume of water (the apparent excess of 3.71 volumes being lost by shrinking upon mixing the alcohol with water). The specific gravity is 0.93353 at 60° F. Thus 86-proof brandy indicates 43 percent alcohol.

The amount of brandy to be added will depend upon three factors: the alcoholic content of the wine, the amount of alcohol in the brandy, and the percent of alcohol desired in the finished product. There is a convenient formula, known as the Pearson Square, which may be employed by the home winemaker. The use of the formula diagramed here consists of five steps:

A D	A. Alcohol content of the spirit you intend to use to fortify the wine.
C	B. Alcohol content of your wine.
	C. Alcohol content you desire.
	D. Difference between B and C.
B E	E. Difference between A and C.

The proportion D to E is the amount to add.

Example

A D	A. 41 percent (82-proof) brandy
41 8	B. 12 percent wine
C	C. 20 percent desired
20	D. 8
B E	E. 21
12 21	The proportion is 8 parts of brandy to 21 parts wine.

When the fortifying brandy is added, it should be well stirred in, for at least five minutes. You may choose to add a little cane sugar for sweetness. Just continue adding the sugar and tasting until desired sweetness is reached. Make sure the sugar is thoroughly stirred into the wine.

Once the wine has been fortified and sweetened, the sherry should then be aged in small (5- to 10-gallon) wooden kegs or barrels. These small wooden containers should be set in your wine cellar for a period of no less than a year. From time to time, take out a little bit of your sherry material and taste it.Remember that a sherry is a wine which has to be overoxidized. This oxidation transforms the alcohol into acetaldehyde, which is the flavor constituent of sherries. As previously stated wooden barrels are porous and allow oxygen to get in and some water to evaporate out. As this oxygen reaches the wine, the oxidation occurs. This takes extensive periods of time and some home winemakers will find that they cannot make a sherry in any less than five or six years. But, in whatever length of time it takes for the sherry to reach its proper taste, the wine should be clarified and stabilized as outlined for white wine production (Chapter 4), and then bottled. (The wine can also be clarified or stabilized just before it is put into the aging containers.) Incidentally, the sherry taste is one that leaves a rather nutlike flavor as an aftertaste.

It should be noted that dry cocktail sherries usually have a percentage of sugar of about 4 percent, a regular sherry about 8 percent, and a cream (crème) sherry will be 12 percent or 13 percent. Dry cocktail sherries are generally very light in color, regular sherries a little darker, and cream sherry quite dark and quite brown. While there are several other methods of commercial production of sherries, none is suitable for the home winemaker's scale of operation.

Port Wine. The operations in the making of port wine are the same as for sherry, except that the wine is almost always selected from very dark red still types. The wine should be stored in a somewhat larger wooden barrel, or even glass or stainless steel containers so that the oxidation effects, or browning, of the smaller keg is not performed as quickly and the red color is preserved. Ports, as well as sherries, must be stored for an extended period of time to produce a proper blending of the brandy with the wine.

The bottles used for dessert wines may have either a cork or a screw-cap closure.

VERMOUTH

Vermouth is a wine flavored with herbs and other aromatic substances. There are two principal types—dry (French type) and sweet (Italian type). The dry is very pale amber and the sweet is dark amber. Vermouth should be made of your lesser-quality wines. For instance, dry white wines, if they have gone a little dark and oxidized and have thus lost most of their fine fresh flavor, can be used to make vermouth.

The wine used for vermouth should be fortified to about 18 to 22 percent of alcohol by volume and a neutral vodka rather than brandy is in order to maintain the light color. If the wine still carries more yellowness than desired, you may add a small amount of activated carbon (see page 107) to lighten it. You must be able to filter this out, however. After the wine is finished—clarified, stabilized, filtered, etc.—the flavoring agents for a vermouth may be added. Herbs used in the flavoring of vermouth are obtainable and very little is needed to give a flavor to the wine. As little as 1 percent of the herbs are soaked in the wine, which is then sweetened according to taste with cane sugar. It is better to soak the herbs in the wine for a day or two rather than in water, as the higher the alcohol concentration is, the more stable the wine will be. It may be of interest to know the ingredients of a vermouth powder and many a home winemaker will like to mix his own herbs. Four ounces of powder, for example, may be made from 1 ounce of dried and powdered balm leaf, 1 ounce of powdered gentian, 1 ounce of fennel seed, a $\frac{1}{4}$ ounce each of yarrow blossom, dried angelica root, dried calamus root, and dried camomile. Traces of cloves, sage, dill seed, ginger, caraway, celery seed, star anise, nutmeg, cinnamon, orange rind, lemon rind, and thyme may also be added, while some vermouth powders also contain spearmint, wintergreen, or peppermint in very small proportions. (Dry vermouth essences already prepared are available from the suppliers listed in Appendix C.) The herbs can be put into a bag and soaked for a few hours with barely enough water to cover them, and then hung for a few days in the wine. An ounce and a half to 2 ounces of herbs to a gallon of wine are suitable.

Sweet vermouth is made in approximately the same way except that the white wine after being fortified will then have small amounts of caramel syrup added to make the wine a light chocolate brown. The wine will then again be clarified, stabilized, and finished in the manner of all dinner wines, and then the flavoring essences added. After your dry and sweet vermouth are finished, they may be bottled with either a cork or screw-cap closure and stored—not necessarily on their sides unless they are corked. Dry vermouth usually has a sugar percentage of about 1 percent; sweet vermouth about 15 percent.

WINE CELLAR

In previous chapters of this book mention has been made of the storage of your wines in the "cellar." This cellar may be part of the home winery or may be located in some other part of the house. In planning the location here are several factors to keep in mind:

Temperature. Wine should not be exposed to temperatures of less than 40° F or more than 80° F. The ideal temperature for the storage of most wines seems to be between 55° and 65° F. When they are kept within a more or less constant temperature range, most wines will mature and improve when stored. They will mature more quickly if kept in warm surroundings, but unless you intend to keep a wine over several years this need not trouble you. Dampness should be guarded against so as to avoid cork mold and label discoloration.

Light. Sunlight is an indispensable friend of the vine, but an implacable enemy of the wine it yields. Susceptibility of some wines to injury by light is the reason many wine bottles are of colored glass. Actually, all bright light is bad, and a wine cellar or storage location should be as dark as possible. No wine, of course, will be damaged by an hour or a day of any light except bright sunlight.

Position. When storing wine, it is important to remember that the temperature close to the floor is much more constant and much cooler than that higher up. Therefore, if you have several racks or bins in your wine cellar or storage location, it's best to keep white dinner wines in the lowest position, sparkling wines on the next lowest, and red dinner on the next. Dessert wines may be stored on top because they are the least affected by higher temperatures. Screw-capped bottles may stand upright; all corked bottles should be laid horizontal or at a slight angle to permit the wine to keep the cork moist. If the cork of a dinner wine dries, the air gets in, the wine then becomes oxidized and gradually spoils. This is also true of champagne. Your dessert wines generally will not spoil because of their being fortified by brandy. The cork of a horizontal bottle in storage should also face frontward, so that if a cork happens to leak you will notice it in time.

Tranquillity. Premium-quality wines you produce merit and should be given respect. If you expect them to improve and mature, subject them to no rough treatment, move them as infrequently as possible, give them the full chance to receive their long, slow, dark, greatly rewarding sleep. In other words, vibrations are another foe of wine. For this reason, do not put wine bottles directly on the floor, but rather keep them on shelves or in racks that are relatively free from vibration. If possible, locate your wine cellar as far away as you can from the constant jarring rumble of trucks, trains, and buses.

Age. One of the virtues of a wine cellar is that many wines improve as they age in the bottle. But if you plan to keep wines for any length of time, there are a few things you ought to know. As we have already seen, each wine ages differently—one reason your own wine cellar is so exciting a hobby. White dinner wines are usually at their best soon after they are bottled, but if storage conditions are favorable they can be kept for a few years before they begin to lose quality. The same can be said for most red dinner wines, too. As a matter of fact, if you do keep a dinner wine in a bottle ten years or more, be very careful since it may have spoiled. Remember, too, that while the life of champagne (and other sparkling wines) is a gay and gallant one, it is quite brief. It is considered "young," or "new," at four years, and quite old at eight or nine. Many people have made the mistake of saving a bottle of champagne for their silver anniversary, only to find it has spoiled during the twenty-five-year interval.

Most dessert wines, on the other hand, continue improving for as many years as you keep them. Just compare a good dessert wine that has been newly bottled with one bottled five years, and note the increased smoothness and flavor. As a rule the longer you store such dessert wines, the better they become.

Construction of the Cellar. After you have selected the location for your wine cellar, the next step is to construct it. A carpenter can make one for you in a few hours. But if you are a do-it-yourselfer why not do the job? One of the wine cellars illustrated should meet your needs. It is, however, impossible to give specific dimensions and material lists since every location where the wine cellar is to be built is different.

It is not necessary to keep your bottles in specially designed racks. They may be placed on a shelf and stacked on top of each other. When this is done, however, a side support or bin arrangement is needed so that the bottles in the bottom row will not roll out from under the weight of the rows on top. The bin arrangement also allows you to keep different types of wine in compartments of their own, young and old wines can be kept apart, and in addition to easy accessibility it permits quick inspection of the bottles for leakage and other possible damage. Over each bin, or compartment, fasten a tag or index card on which such information as the type of wine, the year made, when bottled, etc., is recorded.

When constructing the bins, it is a good idea to put a thin strip of wood (¼ inch thick at the most) under the shoulders of the bottles in the bottom row, so as to give a slight tilt or slant to the entire pile. This is especially recommended for red wines that are to be stored for any length of time, and any wine bottled before it is a year old. This slight slant given to the bottles in storage will cause any sediment to fall beyond the neck and toward the bottom of the bottle, thus permitting easy decanting. But it is *most* important that this slight elevation of the bottle shoulder should not prevent the wine from remaining in constant contact with its cork stopper. If contact between the cork and wine cannot be kept, remove the wood strip and permit the bottles to lie flat on their sides. When wines are racked and fined properly, they throw down little sediment anyway.

In your wine cellar or winery, you should have a wine record book which contains such information relating to the production of a particular batch of wine as type—or types—of grapes used, the vineyard where obtained, time and place of purchase, price, amount of juice extracted per bushel of grapes, date of crushing, date of pressing, vigor of fermentation, length of time in fermenter, amount of sugar added (if any), amount of water added (if any), amount of tannic acid added (if any), dates of racking, date of fining, length of time in storage container, date of bottling, number of bottles filled, and any other information which may be of interest to you. As the years go by, this book, plus fermentation reports, results of various chemical tests, etc., will become an excellent guide to future improvement, as well as an impressive record of past achievement.

Chapter Eight

Using the Fruits of Your Work

Wines are for enjoyment. They bring zest and flavor to favorite foods. They are a superb refreshment. They add pleasure to *all* meals—casual and dinner party alike. If you are proud of your culinary prowess, the wine you serve will enhance your dishes, whether meat, fish, or fowl—and make you even prouder, especially if you have made it yourself.

HOW TO TASTE WINE

Knowing how to "taste" wine is most important to any wine-maker. It will not only help him in turning out a good product, but it is one of the fun parts of the entire winemaking procedure.

The flavor of a wine is a combination of bouquet, aroma, and actual taste to the tongue. Some taste characteristics are definitely describable, such as sweet, sour, bitter, and sharp. Other descriptive terms are "flat," "insipid," and "puckery." However, occasionally terms descriptive of a flavor are used which are at best difficult to define. For instance, take the term "fruity." Is this descriptive of a grape-juice flavor or is it a particular hint of a flavor of an apple or pear or a combination of fruit juices? Another term sometimes used is "flowery." The same wide variations hold true here. (See Appendix A for a full listing of wine-tasting terms.)

The *full* enjoyment of wine calls for the use of the three senses: *sight*—for judging color and clarity; *smell*—for savoring aroma and bouquet; and *taste*—for appreciating the flavor. The overall reaction of the three senses to a given wine is much to be desired in judging a wine. Comments such as "pleasing to the taste" and "appealing in appearance" will tend to reflect ultimate public acceptance of the product. Actually, the hardest task that we commercial winemakers have to face is to make our wines so that other people will like our product; each of our wines is our prized possession and made to our personal tastings, but if you—the public—do not like them, they do us little good. We therefore must produce wines we think that the public will like. You—the home winemaker—have, of course, a much easier task: you have only to please yourself and your family.

Many people take courses in music and art appreciation, and learning the fundamentals of wine tasting can be the equivalent of a course in wine appreciation. If you can discriminate between a mediocre cup of coffee and a good one, you can soon learn to do the same with wine. To help you along in this task, we offer the following wine-tasting suggestions:

1. Pour about one ounce of wine into (preferably) a stemmed glass with a tulip-shaped bowl (an all-purpose glass). Raise the glass to the light; examine for color, brilliance, and clarity.

2. With the glass held between thumb and forefinger, gently swirl the wine in the glass. As you swirl it, sniff the wine's fragrance to get its full aroma and bouquet. (*Aroma* is the fragrance from the grapes; *bouquet*, the fragrance from fermenting and aging.)

3. Take a sip of the wine. Slowly roll it with the tongue to expose it to all the taste buds. Note the pleasant tartness of the dinner wines, the richness and balance of the appetizer and dessert wines. (In succeeding sips, note the sweetness or lack of sweetness, the body or consistency, the distinctive flavor and other characteristics. In your taste memory, try to compare the sensations with other wines you know.)

4. Finally, swallow the wine and enjoy the aftertaste. It does things to your taste buds *after* it is swallowed.

Between sips, and, if you are tasting more than one wine, between wines (always taste from lightest-and-driest wine to sweetest-and-heaviest and usually white to red), clear the palate with a bite of bland cheese, a cracker, or a piece of bread, or take a sip of water.

This, in effect, is the whole process of tasting wines. Memory, of course, has a very important function. To develop a skilled palate, taste frequently and critically, comparing current impressions with memories of other wines you have enjoyed. Although such things as acidity, alcohol percentage, sugar content, etc., can be tested today chemically, it is necessary for experienced tasters to decide such items as color, aroma, flavor, and other qualities. While a wine may be perfect by laboratory test, the practiced palate of an experienced taster can still often find imperfections. Remember that taste is always more important than chemical analysis.

WHICH WINE WITH WHICH FOOD

The question "Which wine goes best with which food?"—although exaggerated by popular belief—should be understood. Just as candy is not eaten with a main course ordinarily, neither is a sweet dessert wine served then. More often, dry dinner wines are enjoyed with main food courses.

Red dinner wines go best with red meats because their more robust flavors blend better with such hearty foods. White dinner wines complement more subtle white meats such as chicken and fish. The characteristic acidity of white dinner wines seems to break down the unpleasant oil substances which give some seafoods "fishy" flavors.

Champagne and rosé are good with all kinds of food. However, perfectionists who recognize that champagne or rosé is always proper show their ignorance by frowning upon the serving of white wine with certain dishes. For the nonperfectionists, but true "connoisseurs," a dry white wine is always acceptable when served all during a meal, as champagne and rosé sometimes are.

The concept that only one wine is exactly right with a particular food is part of the tradition of wine enthusiasts who make wine a lifetime hobby. But millions of daily wine users who enjoy red wines with all foods, or white wines with all foods, are amused at the suggestion that they could be wrong. It boils down to the fact that in wine selection and enjoyment, just as in other areas of good living, personal taste and trial are better guides than rules. If a firm rule were established it might be "The wine that pleases you is the wine to use."

HOW TO SERVE WINE

Just as the question of which wine with which food has become one of personal taste, so have the guidelines for serving wine.

Wine service is easy and simple. There are certain formal wine customs, some of them quite practical. These are considered "in order" only on very special occasions, and even these do not have to be rigid. The important thing is that wine is for pleasure— your pleasure, and that of your guests.

Wines can be served chilled or unchilled, depending on the wine, the weather, or your preference. Actually, bringing the wine to the right temperature is not a long process because—what most people do not realize—wine taken from storage is already not too far from the right temperature. Red wines may need some "warming up," whites and rosés some "cooling down," but both to a lesser extent than is generally believed.

Red wine is generally drunk at what is called "room temperature." When the term "room temperature" (in French "chambre") was coined centuries ago, dining rooms were much cooler than those of today. Huge rooms were heated only by a log fire and, certainly, "room temperature" was never intended to mean the temperature of our present-day, centrally heated dwellings. The right temperature for red wine is about 60° to 65° F. Chilling a red wine will often destroy its character but may somewhat counteract its lack of aging. White and rosé wines are served slightly chilled (around 50° F.) and one hour on the shelf of the refrigerator will bring them to the right temperature. Champagne and other sparkling wines take longer to chill and are left in the refrigerator for a few hours. Champagne, as well as rosé and white wine, may be kept on a lower shelf of the refrigerator.

Opening a wine bottle when a cork closure or stopper is employed should give no real trouble—if you have a *good* corkscrew. While a hundred different types of corkscrews are on the market, generally one responds most effectively to your particular touch. But aside from personal idiosyncrasies, when buying a corkscrew it is best to obtain one that has rounded worm edges, with an open space down the center of the worm and the point exactly in line with the spirals. The most popular type corkscrew with amateur wine connoisseurs—because it is especially good when the cork is old—is the good leverage type which can be purchased in hardware departments or liquor stores.

To actually draw the cork, first, cut the capsule, if you used one,

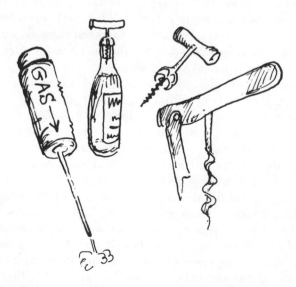

Fig. 27: Types of corkscrews and how to open a bottle with them.

about one-quarter inch below the lip of the bottle. After the top portion of the capsule has been removed, wipe the mouth of the bottle carefully with a napkin. After you have found the center of the cork, turn the point of your corkscrew down all the way through it. (It holds better that way.) The cork itself should be drawn with a gradual pull. Jerking may break it. If you use a good leverage or bell-type corkscrew you can pull the cork while holding the bottle firmly on the table. It is wise to give the corkscrew a *slight* twist or turn to the right when starting to pull. After the cork is drawn, the mouth of the bottle should be wiped clean with a napkin and then the wine can be poured.

Red wine is improved if the bottle is uncorked about one hour before the meal. As we know, wine is a living body. It is dormant in the bottle, and, as soon as the bottle is uncorked, the wine is "awakened" and starts "breathing." It absorbs oxygen from the air and this oxidation activates the development of the bouquet and the aroma. One hour or so of "breathing" gives depth and smoothness to red wine. White and rosé wines have a very delicate fragrance which would lose its freshness if it were exposed to air for too long a time. Therefore the bottles are opened just before serving. Bottles of champagne and sparkling wines are, of course, opened right at the table to prevent the precious bubbles from escaping into the air.

When serving wine, you, as host, traditionally pour the first little bit into your own glass (about one-quarter full) to make sure that the wine is in good condition and to catch any particles of cork which might have fallen into the wine. After tasting it, as a compliment to your guests, you start around the table, to the right (clockwise), filling the glasses of the ladies first, then those of the gentlemen. To be a bit less formal, the glasses may be passed to you, filled, and passed back. (This is proper procedure for any refilling of your guests' glasses.) Or, if you wish, pass the bottle on down the table for the others to help themselves. In any case, after all your guests' glasses have been filled, you should fill your own. At a buffet dinner, the host should again pour the first glass of wine even though the bottles are generally left on the sideboard and the guests help themselves.

The wine is usually poured after the food has been served. Remember that glasses should be left on the table—not lifted—for

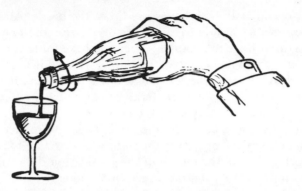

Fig. 28: Proper method of pouring wine.

filling, and they should never be filled more than three-fourths full—a bit more than halfway is better. If two wines are to be served, the lighter and drier one usually comes first. Don't serve wines of different types in the same glass.

The best way to avoid dripping wine on the tablecloth is to give the wine bottle a slight twist to the right before raising its mouth from the pouring position, thus catching the last few drops on the lip of the bottle. It is not necessary or desirable to wrap a napkin around a chilled wine bottle when pouring. Merely wipe the bottle dry before opening. Also superfluous is the ice bucket or cooler at the table for chilled white table wines. If the bottle is brought to the table properly chilled at the beginning, it can remain on the table for easy, non-messy handling. It is advisable to set the bottle on a bread-and-butter plate, or some other small plate, in order to save the tablecloth. You might use a regular bottle coaster.

Do not serve the wine from some place remote from the dining table. The opened wine bottle should be kept at the host's right. Do not try to whisk it away as soon as it is empty. Wine bottles are interesting in themselves, and decorative as well. They add atmosphere to your table. You also compliment your guests by "showing off" the bottle of wine you are serving for their enjoyment. After all, it is a product of your "labor of love."

A question very often asked is "How many servings in a bottle?" The chart on the opposite page answers this question. The average serving of dinner wine or champagne is usually 4 to 6 fluid ounces; of appetizer or dessert wine, 2 to 2½ ounces. These bottles give you these approximate servings:

Size	Ounces	Dinner Wines, Champagne	Dessert Wines
Fifth (4/5 qt.)	25.6	4-6 servings	8-12 servings
Tenth (4/5 pt.)	12.8	2-3 servings	4-6 servings
Split	6.4	2 servings	
Quart	32.0	6-8 servings	10-14 servings
Pint	16.0	3-4 servings	5-7 servings
½ gallon	64.0	12-16 servings	20-30 servings
Gallon	128.0	24-30 servings	40-60 servings

In addition to these popular sizes, extra-large bottles, sometimes used for special occasions, include the magnum (52 oz.); the double magnum, or jeroboam (104 oz.); the tappit-hen (128 oz.); the rehoboam (156 oz.); the methuselah (208 oz.); the salmanazar (312 oz.); the balthazar (416 oz.); and the nebuchadnessar (520 oz.). With the exception of the magnum, these bottles are difficult to obtain. Owing to the use of the metric system of measurement in Europe, many foreign wine bottles, though similar in shape and appearance to the standard American "fifth," contain 24 U.S. liquid ounces, rather than the 25.6 ounces required by law for a "fifth" bottle filled in the United States.

Opening a Champagne Bottle. If you have used a foil capsule on your champagne bottle, cut it around the bottle neck down about 1½ inches from the top and remove the upper part. Then grasp the wire loop and unwind it. This permits the wire hood to be removed from the cork and bottle. Next grasp the mushroom top of the champagne cork firmly, holding the thumb over the top so it will not get away from you and strike someone should it pop too soon. (If you are right-handed, the right thumb will be over the cork.) Hold the lower part of the bottle in the other hand. Now turn the bottle slowly in one direction, keeping it at an angle of about 45°. (Remember that an angled bottle will not overflow so readily as an upright one. But have a glass handy just in case.) Twist the bottle, not the cork, that's the expert's

Fig. 29: How to open a champagne bottle.

secret. The section of the husky champagne cork in the bottle has a paraffined outer layer, put there to help you. If the internal pressure does not push the cork out, work the cork from side to side. Hold on to the cork as it leaves the bottle.

After the cork is out, keep the bottle at the 45° angle for a few seconds, or a count of ten, before you bring the bottle to a vertical position. This permits the pressure within the bottle to equalize itself with that outside the bottle and will prevent the wine from bubbling over. The actual pouring is done in two motions. Pour the champagne until the froth almost reaches the brim of the glass. Stop. Wait a moment until this foaming froth subsides, then continue pouring to fill the glass two-thirds to three-fourths full. Be careful not to pour too rapidly or the wine will froth over the lip of the glass. To prevent dripping, turn the bottle slowly to the right as you raise it from the glass. The bottle should be returned to the cooler or ice bucket after each pouring to keep the sparkling wine cold and thus preserve the effervescence.

Glasses for champagne should be completely dry before a drop is poured. In other words, chill the wine—not the glass. And never add ice cubes to a glass of champagne.

Decanting Wine. When you keep red wines for years, you

may find a sediment, crust or film (sometimes called *chemise*) deposited on the sides or bottoms of the bottles. Such a sediment from over the years in red wines is usually a proud mark of age and will settle if the bottle is allowed to rest half an hour. While the sediment is harmless, the wine may be decanted before serving in order to avoid pouring it into the guests' glasses.

If you ever have occasion to perform the decanting rite, it should be done at least a half to three-quarters of an hour before serving, to give the wine a chance to breathe, which is the second good reason for decanting. (Young wines develop in the presence of air, seeming to lose any tendency to hardness, which is one reason why so many fruity wines seem to taste better as the meal progresses.) The actual decanting operation is merely the pouring of the wine gently and steadily from the old bottle into another bottle, carafe, or pitcher. It is usually done with a candle or other light behind the bottleneck, so that the clarity of the wine may be watched and pouring stopped as soon as the sediment appears.

Another way to avoid putting sediment into your guests' glasses is to lay the bottle in a metal or wickerware cradle or wine basket, which is especially designed to hold it horizontal during the carrying and opening procedures. The wine bottle to be served in a basket should be lifted from the storage or bin in exactly the same position in which it has lain, and should be deposited in the cradle in that position. The bottle in the basket should not be shaken and should be allowed to rest on the table until any sediment aroused in the moving has settled. A corkscrew that uses leverage is best when you have to extract the cork from a bottle lying in a cradle. When the wine is poured, it should be done very gently so that the deposit remains at the bottom. The last half glass of wine is left in the bottle if not clear. Some "connoisseurs" prefer to decant an old red wine into another bottle before serving, but they proudly exhibit the original crusted bottle to their guests. It is not usually necessary to decant white wines, as they rarely have a heavy sediment.

WHEN WINE IS LEFT OVER

Unlike the before-opening storing techniques for wine previously given, there is no set rule of thumb on their storage after opening. Once opened, all wines should be used as soon as possible. Contact with air and heat does not improve the wine. It is better to be overcautious than to be disappointed in wine that has been stored poorly or too long. The following general precautions should be taken with wine remaining from table or cooking use:

Dessert Wines. Once opened, these wines keep well for weeks unless they are exposed to air for very long periods. Spoilage often can be traced to the hospitable host who hesitates to recap the bottle at the table, lest he seems to grudge a second serving. It is generally stated that dessert wines can be "kept at room temperature." Which room, what temperature? A kitchen cupboard or closet shelf can be hot; the wine suffers in silence. Therefore, have a cool storage spot for opened bottles of dessert wines.

Dinner Wines. Because of their lower alcoholic content, dinner wines are perishable after opening. For this reason, wines of this type—both red and white—should be used in their entirety at a meal or as quickly as possible after use.

When you have opened a gallon or half-gallon jug of *red* dinner wine and have used only part of the contents, and if you do not plan to finish it within a few days, transfer it to smaller bottles to use later. Use clean screw-cap bottles and follow the general decanting procedure. Fill to three-quarters or one inch from the top, to allow for expansion.

When you plan to use the leftover dinner wine only for cooking, you can keep it much longer by just adding enough olive oil to form a thin film on the wine, then closing the bottle tightly. Such wines are best used in meat, poultry, and fish cookery, not in desserts or with fruit.

Sparkling Wines. Once the cork is out, it is rather difficult to hold the lively bubbles in the wine. The design of some champagne bottles allows them to be recapped with bottle stoppers. If this is done, the wine must be kept well chilled. (If the champagne loses its effervescence, it can still be employed in cooking in the same manner as a white dinner wine. The loss of its bubbles doesn't affect its value as a cooking wine.) Chilled, unopened bottles of sparkling wines may be transferred to regular storage without loss of flavor.

WINE GLASSES

Wine is for beauty, too, and stemmed glassware does more for its beauty than an ordinary kitchen tumbler. Even so, millions will contend that wine is wine, whatever the glass.

The all-purpose glass, suited to any wine served, has gained much popularity in recent years. A glass of this type is clear crystal, stemmed, and without color or ornamentation to distract from the wine. The stem is for a practical purpose—to serve as a sort of handle. When the glass is held by the stem the heat of the hand will not warm the wine. The bowl should have about a six- to eight-ounce capacity. This permits a generous serving but also allows room for the aroma and fragrance to collect above the wine, where it may be sniffed and enjoyed.

This glass is ideal for dinner wines and, in fact, for any wine. The connoisseur, in addition to these glasses for his red dinner wines, would perhaps have different-style glasses for his white dinner wines, champagnes, and appetizer and dessert wines. A white wine glass has a longer stem than the all-purpose glass, but a slightly smaller bowl. Champagne glasses are of two types: a stemmed, flat, saucer style, or the tulip-shaped, similar to, but

Fig. 30: Some of the more common wine glasses.

taller and slimmer than those used for dinner wines. They sometimes are designed with hollow stems, which many people believe tend to accentuate the natural effervescence of sparkling wines.

Dessert wines generally are served in short-stemmed glasses with a tulip-shaped bowl holding about three ounces. A special glass frequently preferred for sherry has a V-shaped, or conical, bowl. Tall glasses such as those used for mixed drinks are appropriate for wine coolers.

WINE FOR COOKING

More and more persons are joining the ranks of professional chefs who would not think of cooking without wine. Wine can mean the difference between tasteless and zestful dishes. The same factors that cause wines to harmonize with foods on the table—their ability to balance the sweetness, acidity, saltiness, and bitterness of food—hold true when wine is used in cooking.

In cooking, the alcoholic content of the wine is completely lost through heat; only the tantalizing aroma and flavor of the wine are imparted to the food. Anyone can cook with wine by simply adding a dash of it when other seasonings are used. Any wine is suitable for cooking use. In the average home, wine left from the table often is used in the kitchen. We suggest that you purchase a copy of *Treasury of Wine and Wine Cookery* by Greyton H. Taylor (Harper & Row) for excellent wine-cooking recipes.

MEDICINAL AND FOOD VALUES OF WINE

Federal law prevents advertising the contribution that wine makes to health, but the contribution has been well established for many centuries. By Biblical times, its medicinal values had already been recognized, since it is recorded in I Timothy: "Drink no longer water, but use a little wine for thy stomach's sake and thine often infirmities."

The people of those days recognized the medicinal values of wine without knowing what produced them. Today scientific and medical research has shown these values are attributable to many substances in wine: vitamins B_1, B_2, and C; iron, calcium, and phosphorus, the blood and bone-building minerals, and thirteen other mineral elements recognized as essential to maintaining animal and human life. While wine has been used in medical practice since earliest times, we must remember that an entire generation of physicians lost touch with many of its important medical uses in the United States during the Prohibition period. These uses are only now beginning to be recognized again in the new era of experimental medicine, in which the exact values of all therapeutic substances must be carefully measured by painstaking scientific research. Working hand-in-hand, various medical groups and the wine industry are finding such important information as the action of wine upon the digestive organs, its use in diseases of the gastrointestinal system; its action upon the kidneys and urinary passages; its use in diseases of the kidneys; its use in diabetes, in infectious diseases, in treatment of the aged and convalescent, and as a base for tonics; and its action upon the cardiovascular, respiratory, nervous, and muscular systems. A great deal of vital data has already been discovered to help mankind, and more is promised in the near future. The great nineteenth-century chemist Louis Pasteur called wine "the healthiest and most hygienic beverage in the world."

Containing as it does all of these health-giving qualities, wine comes in many different guises—a tonic, an appetizer, a digestive, a quick energizer, and a nutrient. In addition, wine with a meal produces a relaxed feeling in the diners. They eat more slowly and enjoy their meal more. Another plus value of wine as a food, especially to weight-conscious individuals, is its low caloric content.

There is an easy way to determine the caloric count of drinks. In dry wines, multiply the alcohol by volume by 1.5; the number obtained equals the number of calories in one ounce. Thus most red, pink, and white wines, as well as champagne, range from 16 to 26 calories per fluid ounce, while dessert wines climb to 36 to 48 calories. Looking further afield at all spirits: the proof equals the number of calories in an ounce.

It is only proper to point out that normal diets—whether for gaining or losing weight—put the emphasis on moderation. As the ancient and modern beverage of moderation, wines certainly can claim a place in anyone's dietary scheme of things.

Chapter Nine

Growing Your Own Grapes

For one to receive the greatest possible pleasure from winemaking, a person should grow his own grapes. By doing this, you can proudly state on your label "Estate Bottled"—a designation given to a wine that was produced and bottled on the vineyard property where the grapes were grown. More important to your wine, however, is the fact that you have the best possible control over the raw material of winemaking—the grapes. And, as was stated in Chapter 3, the chief cause of poor wine is poor grapes.

It does not take a great acreage to produce enough wine for the average household use. On a plot of land 100 by 100 feet, it is possible to get enough grapes to produce about 130 gallons of wine a year. Following general viticultural practices, you can set out on this size plot as many as 14 rows of 14 vines each, or 196 vines. Annual yields will vary a good deal, but assuming 8 pounds per vine the annual yield will amount to over 1,500 pounds. Then, figuring that 12 pounds of grapes equals about 1 gallon of juice, we find that the 100-by-100-foot plot will produce enough raw materials for about 130 gallons of wine. With some high-yield grapes, this figure would be increased, and you can plant several species in the same home vineyard.

SELECTING GRAPE VARIETIES

As was stated in Chapter 3, there are three major types or families of grape varieties: the American grapes, European-American grapes, and the *vinifera* varieties. The problem for the prospective viticulturist is to determine which are most likely to provide him with the wine he wants—what wine grapes, in short, are most promising in his particular environment.

Any system of districts—for example, the one shown on the map (Fig. 31)—must be considered highly tentative, and must be based on such broad grounds that it is subject to numerous exceptions and qualifications. Actually, we cannot emphasize too strongly that this scheme of districts must not be taken literally, either as to its boundaries, the details of the following descriptive notes, or the recommendations of varieties for planting. The wine characteristics of many of the following varieties are given in Chapter 3. (Note: Species marked with an asterisk are suitable for table or raisin use.)

DISTRICT NO. 1

White	Red-Blue-Black
Seyval (Seyve-Villard 5276)	Baco Noir (Baco No. 1)
Delaware	Landal (Landot 244)
Dutchess	Chambourcin (Johannes-Seyve 26-205)
Catawba	Chelois (Seibel 10878)
Ravat Blanc (Ravat 6)	Florental (Burdin 7705)
Aurora (Seibel 5279)	Bath

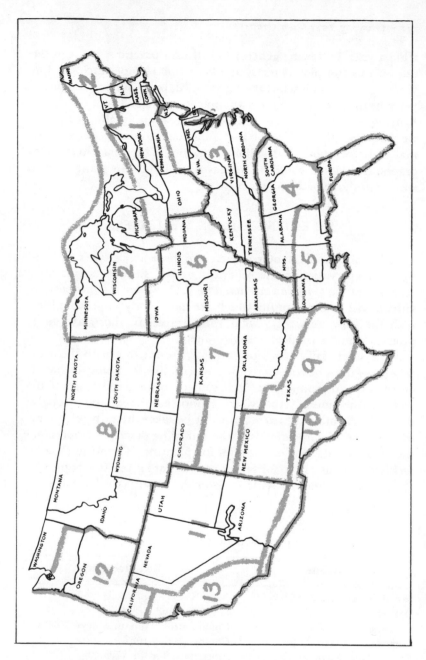

Fig. 31: The grape-growing districts of the United States.

DISTRICT NO. 1 (*continued*)

White	Red-Blue-Black
Diamond	Buffalo
Elvira	Maréchal Foch
Vidal 256	Léon Millot
*Niagara	*Concord

This district contains most of the principal *present* grape-growing sections outside of District 13. Characterized by low winter temperatures and rather short growing season, except where near larger bodies of water. On the shores of important lakes in this district are the largest acreages of American grapes.

DISTRICT NO. 2

White		Red-Blue-Black
Elvira		⌠Janesville
Aurora (S-5279)	To try in	│Baco Noir (Baco No. 1)
*Niagara	Southern	│Ironclad
	part of	│Bacchus
	District	│Alpha
		⌡Clinton
		Beta
		Campbell Early
		Worden
		Red Amber
		Bluejay
		*Concord

Characterized by extremely low winter temperatures. Has the shortest growing season of any district in the country. Only very hearty varieties are worthy of trial.

DISTRICT NO. 3

White	Red-Blue-Black
Seyval (Seyve-Villard 5276)	Baco Noir (Baco No. 1)
Delaware	Landal (Landot 244)

DISTRICT NO. 3 *(continued)*

White	Red-Blue-Black
Dutchess	Chambourcin (Johannes-Seyve 26-205)
Catawba	Chelois (Seibel 10878)
Ravat Blanc (Ravat 6)	Florental (Burdin 7705)
Aurora (Seibel 5279)	Bath
Diamond	Buffalo
Elvira	Maréchal Foch
Vidal 256	Léon Millot
*Niagara	*Concord
Pinot Chardonnay ⎱ Southern ⎰ Pinot Noir	
Johannisberger Riesling ⎰ Section ⎱ Cabernet	

This area grows quite a bit of *Vitis muscadinia,* of which is included the famous Scuppernong. Soil and climate conditions vary greatly in this district. We recommend here grafting varieties on Malegue 44.53 or Couderc 3309 rootstock.

DISTRICT NO. 4

White	Red-Blue-Black
Seyval (Seyve-Villard 5276)	Landal (Landot 244)
Delaware	Chambourcin (Johannes-Seyve 26-205)
Dutchess	Chelois (Seibel 10878)
Catawba	Florental (Burdin 7705)
Ravat Blanc (Ravat 6)	Bath
Aurora (Seibel 5279)	Buffalo
Diamond	Maréchal Foch
Vidal 256	*Concord
Pinot Chardonnay	Cabernet Sauvignon
Johannisberger Riesling	Pinot Noir

Long hot summers and also great differences in winter climate and soils. Grafting on Malegue 44.53 is recommended.

DISTRICT NO. 5

White	Red-Blue-Black
Seyval (Seyve-Villard 5276)	Villard Noir (Seyve-Villard 18-315)
Roucaneuf (Seyve-Villard 12-309)	Maréchal Foch
Delaware	Chambourcin (Johannes-Seyve 26.205)
Dutchess	Landal (Landot 244)
Pinot Chardonnay	Cabernet Sauvignon
Johannisberger Riesling	Pinot Noir
	Delicatessen

This area is sometimes rather profuse in soil nematodes and here Malegue 44.53 rootstocks are particularly recommended. Muscadine have been the leading grape varieties in this section.

DISTRICT NO. 6

White	Red-Blue-Black
Seyval (Seyve-Villard 5276)	Landal (Landot 244)
Delaware	Chambourcin (Johannes-Seyve 26-205)
Dutchess	Chelois (Seibel 10878)
Catawba	Florental (Burdin 7705)
Ravat Blanc (Ravat 6)	Bath
Aurora (Seibel 5279)	Buffalo
Diamond	Maréchal Foch
Vidal 256	* Concord
Roucaneuf (Seyve-Villard 12-309)	America
	Champanel
	Neva Munson
	Black Rose
	Delicatessen

Rather hot summers, fairly cold winters. Varies from rather high mountain areas to flat or rolling prairies, which include many of the country's more important rivers, on the banks of which considerable grape growing is done.

DISTRICT NO. 7

White	Red-Blue-Black
Seyval (Seyve-Villard 5276)	Baco Noir (Baco No. 1)
Delaware	Landal (Landot 244)
Catawba	Chambourcin (Johannes-Seyve 26-205)
Ravat Blanc (Ravat 6)	Chelois (Seibel 10878)
Aurora (Seibel 5279)	Florental (Burdin 7705)
Diamond	Bath
Elvira	Buffalo
Vidal 256	Léon Millot
*Niagara	*Concord

Also suggest Kandaia, Ruby, and Athens. This district has rather severe winters, but a moderately long growing season. Land characterized by rolling open country.

DISTRICT NO. 8

White	Red-Blue-Black
Elvira	Janesville
Aurora (S-5279)	Baco Noir (Baco No. 1)
*Niagara	Ironclad
	Bacchus
	Alpha
	Clinton
	Beta
	Campbell Early
	Worden
	Red Amber
	Bluejay
	*Concord

Add as possibilities in warmer regions of this district:

White	Red-Blue-Black
Delaware	Chelois (Seibel 10878)
Seyval (Seyve-Villard S-276)	Léon Millot
Diamond	

Largest of the districts. Cold winter temperature. Dry winds, many parts having very limited rainfall. No particular part well adapted to grape growing and only very hearty varieties have a chance of succeeding.

DISTRICT NO. 9

White	Red-Blue-Black
Seyval (Seyve-Villard 5276)	Landal (Landot 244)
Delaware	Chambourcin (Johannes-Seyve 26-205)
Dutchess _	Chelois (Seibel 10878)
Catawba	Florental (Burdin 7705)
Ravat Blanc (Ravat 6)	Maréchal Foch
Aurora (Seibel 5279)	America
Roucaneuf (Seyve-Villard 12-309)	Champanel
	Neva Munson
	Black Rose
	Delicatessen

High altitude. Limited rainfall.

DISTRICT NO. 10

White	Red-Blue-Black
*Sultania (Thompson Seedless)	Black Hamburg
	Mission

Probably the poorest grape-growing district. Winter temperatures do not get very low. Almost certainly need irrigation. Would recommend here particularly to consult area horticultural centers.

DISTRICT NO. 11

White	Red-Blue-Black
Delaware—northern	* Concord
Aurora (Seibel 5279)—southern	Isabella
*Niagara—northern	Baco Noir (Baco No. 1)
Elvira—northern	Landal (Landot 244)

DISTRICT NO. 11 *(continued)*

White	Red-Blue-Black
Catawba—northern	Chambourcin (Johannes-Seyve 26-205)
Seyval (Seyve-Villard 5276)— southern	Zinfandel
Pinot Chardonnay	Léon Millot
	Chelois (Seibel 10878)

May need irrigation in southern part of this district. Commercial grape growing should certainly not be attempted; however, amateur viticulturists may have a good chance of growing grapes in the irrigated localities free of alkali.

DISTRICT NO. 12

White	Red-Blue-Black
Delaware	Campbell Early
Diamond	Zinfandel
Seyval (Seyve-Villard 5276)	Black Hamburg
Elvira	Worden
Aurora (Seibel 5279)	Léon Millot
Pinot Chardonnay	Baco Noir (Baco No. 1)

In recent years, this district has shown a great deal of promise for commercial grape growing.

DISTRICT NO. 13

White	Black
Seyval (Seyve-Villard 5276)	Chambourcin (Johannes-Seyve 26-205)
Catawba	Maréchal Foch
Ravat Blanc (Ravat 6)	Landal (Landot 244)
Pinot Chardonnay	Cabernet Sauvignon
Johannisberger Riesling	Pinot Noir
Palomino	Zinfandel
Gewürztraminer	Gamay
French Colombard	

Largest grape producer in the United States. In most areas other than the Napa and Somona valleys, irrigation will be necessary. We suggest you contact the University of California at Davis for further information on grape growing in District 13.

There are several excellent reference books that amateur grape growers should have in their wine library: *The Grapes of New York* by U. P. Hedrick (information applies to Districts 1, 2, 3, 7, 8, 11, and 12); *Foundations of American Grape Culture* by T. V. Munson (information applies to Districts 3, 4, 5, 6, 7, 8, 9, 11, and 12); *California Wine Grapes* by M. A. Amerine and A. J. Winkler (applies only to District 13); *A Wine-Grower's Guide* by P. M. Wagner (general book—applies to all districts); and *General Viti-culture* by A. J. Winkler (general book—applies to all districts).

SELECTION OF VINEYARD SITE

A desirable vineyard site should have adequate air drainage (free from trees and bushes), moderate degree of slope, and a deep, well-drained soil. An adequate site with the proper soil conditions will produce large, vigorous vines which will return big yields. Shallow soil with poor drainage will produce weak vines. For this reason, vines set on poorly or slowly drained soils should be planted closer together in the rows in order to make use of the entire trellis area.

As soon as possible after the selection of a site for planting, it is advisable to consult your county agricultural agent about taking a soil sample and having a complete analysis made. The results of such an analysis can be used as a guide in preparing the soil before the roots are actually planted. Your county agricultural agent should also be consulted in interpreting the results of an analysis.

If there is any reason to believe, or the soil analysis shows, that the organic matter in the soil is low, every effort should be made to build this up by the addition and incorporation of such ma-terials as manure, cured hay or straw, wood chips, sawdust, etc. Nitrogen should be added to any of the other materials, with the exception of manure, at the time of the incorporation with the soil. Green cover crops, such as clover, turned under will con-tribute to the soil organic matter, but not to the extent that liberal applications of dry, ripe material such as straw or cured hay will.

Because spring is the best time to plant vines in most parts of our country, the soil should be turned over thoroughly in the fall. This will allow time for the partial breakdown of any cover crop being turned under, which might seriously interfere with the planting operation if done in the spring. If practical to do so, some means of protection can be given the ground during the winter. A very thin layer of straw or old hay spread over the turned-over ground for protection from erosion can be very easily disked into the soil in the spring without interfering with the planting operation. Even if it is not possible adequately to protect a vineyard area during the winter months, it is still better to turn the ground over in the fall. A large amount of unrotted organic matter in the soil will greatly lengthen the time involved in hand planting.

PURCHASING YOUR VINES

When selecting the varieties and vines for your home vineyard, keep the following in mind:

1. Yield and composition of the grapes under your soil and climatic conditions.

2. Inherent vigor of the vine.

3. Scion-stock interrelationships. In many areas, desirable varieties must be grafted to soil-adapted rootstock.

4. Susceptibility to disease.

5. The influence of environmental conditions—rainfall, wind, fog, humidity, exposure, mean daily temperature, time of maturity.

6. The basic quality of the wine produced by the variety.

It is well, in making preliminary plans, to take a look through the vineyards of your region, noting the excellences and the faults. Seek the advice of the owners of good plantings. The United States Department of Agriculture, agricultural colleges, state experiment stations, and the county agent also give help that is almost indispensable in making selections of vines, as well as on the entire subject of grape growing. Still another source of information and inspiration is the nurseryman's catalog. From these sources, plus the recommended species given earlier in this chapter, you should be able to select the best varieties for your vine-yard.

When purchasing the vines, select the best possible ones from a reliable nurseryman. (We have listed several in Appendix C.) The grapevines normally available to the grower for planting are sold under the followng grades:

The grade 1-X represents the very best grade of one-year-old vines grown during the past season. These are the "cream of the crop" and the number available each year is limited. Vines of this grade have consistently outgrown vines of the other grades and matured a year ahead of them. The premium price asked for 1-X grade vines is well worth paying.

The grade 1-1 represents the best average grade of one-year-old vines grown during the past season which have a good dense, sub-stantial root growth. The largest portion of the vines grown each year will be of this grade, providing growing conditions are op-timum. The 1-1 grade vines are highly recommended for planting.

The grade 1-2 represents the one-year-old vines with the top and root growth just below average. This grade of vine can be successfully used for planting, but will be slower in coming into bearing than the 1-1 grade vines. If the 1-X and 1-1 grade vines are available, they should be purchased in preference to the 1-2 grade vines.

The one-year-old vines which have made the poorest top and root growth are termed "culls." The abundance of culls in the nursery in any one year can depend on several factors. Poor wood used for cutting material will result in vines of cull grade. However, unsatisfactory top and root growth are not necessarily the result of this. A wet, cool growing season will result in a large number of culls due to insufficient root growth regardless of how good the cuttings were at the time of planting in the nursery. A very dry growing season will also cause the number of culls to be proportionately greater.

The best of the culls from the one-year-old vines and the grade 1-2 vines not sold on the market are planted in the nursery the following spring and permitted to develop an additional season. When these are removed from the ground in the late fall and graded, the most vigorous vines are sold on the market as grade 2-1. This grade of vine is satisfactory for planting providing that the root growth is dense, vigorous, and compact. In purchasing vines of this grade, the grower should not accept vines with a long, coarse root system, nor should he accept vines with a scanty root system. A general recommendation can be made to all growers, regardless of the variety and grade they are buying: be sure that the vines have a good, substantial, healthy, and sound root system.

It is not difficult to propagate your own rootings from cuttings. This can be done to expand your vineyard from your own vines or obtain stock from vines that particularly interest you. The simplest way to do this is to make cuttings with three buds from the varieties you want while the wines are dormant. The cuttings are bound in bundles, kept cool and moist, and dug in sand or sawdust until spring. Then they are trenched into the ground with only the top bud exposed. If cultivated with a hoe or trowel and kept in moist soil, the cutting will develop roots and foliage that can be handled as regular nursery stock in the fall.

A few precocious vines bear fruit two years after being set in the vineyard; most varieties bear at three years; and a few do not begin to bear until they have been planted four years. None, of course, come to full bearing until several years later. These ages are modified by soil, climate, and the care given the vines, though nature cannot be hurried greatly by man.

PLANTING A VINEYARD

The difficulties of planting a home vineyard are greatly exaggerated. If the land is properly prepared, and the vines in good condition, planting is easily, safely, and quickly done. For instance, the slope of the land largely determines the direction of rows. On sloping land, rows should follow the drainage grade laid out by local soil conservation technicians. Such a planting plan is the best way to prevent or reduce erosion and to preserve the site for the long life of the vineyard. Rows at right angles to the slope (cross-slope planting) are a better arrangement than rows parallel to the slope, and when the vineyard consists of both slope and level ground it is also best to run the rows at right angles to the slope.

Space needed by power equipment, if you plan to use it, largely governs the distance between rows in the vineyard. Rows spaced

7 or 8 feet apart allow ample room for any home vineyard power equipment—tractors and sprayers—now in use. It is suggested that vines be set 8 feet apart in the row. However, in experiments highest yields have been obtained at closer spacings, especially between rows. If low vigor is anticipated, vines should be planted closer than 8 feet apart in the row to get more plants in a given area and higher yields.

There are many ways to mark the field. If it is to be planted along a drainage grade, the curved rows are already marked. To get straight rows, you can drive a white stake at each corner of the proposed planting, then drive other stakes at 7- or 8-foot intervals between the corner stakes, using a 7- or 8-foot pole to measure. By keeping the end stakes in line with the corner stakes, the pole affords an easy way to space the rows. A pole the length of the vine spacing can be used in the row to space each vine as it is planted.

In setting grapevines, these essentials should be kept in mind:

1. All the roots that are alive and sound should be retained and kept moist and cool until covered by soil.

2. All these roots should be set 12 to 15 inches deep, be reasonably spread, and be firmly packed with friable soil. The union of grafted vines should be several inches above the vineyard floor.

Within these conditions, a wide array of planting techniques is successful. Usually, planting is done by hand in a furrow. The vine spacing is measured by a pole of the correct length, or by a planting wire marked at appropriate distances and stretched along the furrow. It is inadvisable to put any fertilizer in the furrow or hole at planting time because of the danger of injuring the roots.

The top of the new vine should be pruned to the best single cane and this should be pruned to two or three buds. When the new shoots are no more than one inch long, all except the two topmost are broken off to promote growth in height. If the 1-inch shoots cannot be broken off at the proper time, the best cane should be pruned to two buds at planting time. If fruit clusters develop, they should be removed in early summer.

A major cost in establishing a vineyard is the trellis. It should be constructed during the first growing season or the following spring; further delay will postpone the harvesting of profitable crops. All vertical trellises for commercial vineyards in New York, for example, are of the same general type: two or three wires, one above the other, stretched tightly on firmly set posts. Two wires are adequate for umbrella Kniffin and 4-arm Kniffin, the most common systems, but three wires are necessary for some other training systems. For vine vigor that is at least average, the top wire of the trellis should be 5½ to 6 feet above the ground to provide good exposure to sunlight and to facilitate insect and disease control. The bottom wire should be 2½ to 3 feet above the ground. Comparisons of yields of vigorous vines on trellises 4 feet high with those 5½ feet high have shown significantly higher yield and higher soluble solids from vines on the higher trellises. These increases were noted only if the vines were sufficiently vigorous to cover the trellis completely with foliage in August.

Posts serve two functions. The intermediate or line posts provide vertical support for the trellis wires. Although the end posts support the wire, too, their main purpose is to provide anchor points for tightening the wires.

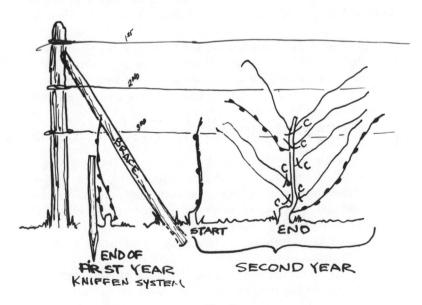

Fig. 32

CARE OF A VINEYARD

Most owners of home vineyards take up wine-grape growing as an avocation and, as amateurs, must learn the secrets of management of vines. One of the first things you should learn is the definitions of vine parts, which are as follows:

Trunk. The main unbranched body or stem of the vine.

Arms. The main branches or extensions of the trunk.

Head. The region of the trunk from which the arms or canes arise.

Old wood. Any part of the vine older than one year.

Shoots. New leafy growths developing from buds. They are called "shoots" during the growing season. After the leaves fall, they become "canes."

Spur. A cane cut back to a short stub, consisting of from one to three buds, to produce next year's fruiting cane at a desired location.

Nodes. The joints on shoots or canes where leaves and buds are attached.

Internodes. The wood of shoots or canes between the nodes.

Suckers. The shoots arising from below the ground.

Water sprouts. The shoots arising from buds along the trunk. Commonly, but mistakenly, referred to as "suckers" by growers.

Cane. A mature woody shoot after leaf fall.

Cordon. The long arm or arms of a vine trained along a wire. When fully developed, the cordon bears canes, renewal spurs, and water sprouts.

Lateral. A branch of a shoot. It may be less than one inch or more than four feet long. The long ones may become mature and woody, and after leaf fall they are called *Lateral canes.*

Bud. A compressed shoot.

Primary. The largest bud or shoot at each normal node of the cane or spur.

Secondary. The basal and the second-largest bud or shoot at each normal node of the cane or spur.

Tendril. A long, slender, curled structure borne at some of the nodes of a shoot. It can firmly attach the shoot to a support.

Petiole. The stem portion of a leaf.

Soil management. The newly planted vineyard should be fertilized each year including the year of planting. Shortly after planting and again early in the second growing season, ring the vines with a high analysis fertilizer such as 10-5-10 at the rate of 2 ounces per vine, or 15-5-15 at the rate of 1½ ounces per vine, or ammonium nitrate at the rate of ¾ ounce per vine. Do not sow a nitrogen fertilizer around the young vines later in the growing season as such a procedure may prolong the period of shoot growth, resulting in immature canes when the leaves drop,

The leaves of the young vines should be periodically checked throughout each growing season for potassium and other deficiencies. We advise you to check your state university horticulture department if your suspicions of disease are aroused.

It is very difficult to correct potash deficiency in young vineyards owing to the fact that the feeder roots are deeper at this stage of growth than later in life. For this reason, it is very important to correct potash deficiency in the soil, as determined by soil analysis, before the vines are planted. You do this either by application just before turning the soil over in the fall or by drilling the potash in before fitting the soil. Nitrogen should be applied to the soil of your vineyard in the third growing season.

Until the trellis is erected, the young vineyard should be cross-cultivated to eliminate weed growth in the rows and between the vines. Hand hoeing around the vines will keep down weed growth that is not controlled with tractor machinery. In the latter part of July of the planting year, work the soil toward the vines with a plow, reversed grape hoe blade, or a disc to form a ridge for the protection of the vines. After the trellis has been constructed, the young vineyard should be cultivated in the same manner as an older vineyard, eliminating weed competition during that part of the growing season when the vines will be making the greatest shoot growth, and stopping cultivation in mid- to late July.

Pruning and Training. Pruning is the act of removing superfluous parts of a plant. In viticulture, the term usually refers to the removal of canes during the dormant season, but it can also refer to growing-season pruning of shoots and root pruning. Dormant-season pruning is done primarily to regulate the quantity and hence quality of the crop, and the growth; the degree or severity of this pruning of canes can be described by the number

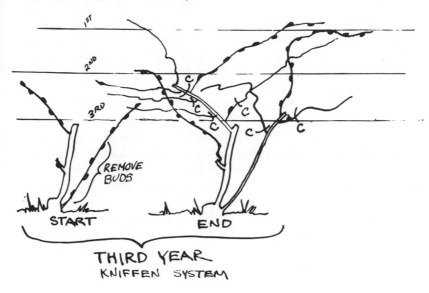

THIRD YEAR
KNIFFEN SYSTEM

Fig. 33

of nodes retained per vine. Consider an unpruned Concord vine whose estimated pruning weight was 4 pounds, with 600 nodes; severe pruning would remove 570 nodes and leave only 30; light pruning would remove only 520 nodes and leave 80; balance pruning at 30 + 10, would take 540 nodes and leave 60. These 60 nodes can be retained on 3-node spurs, 4- to 7-node short canes, or 8- to 15-node canes. These three degrees of pruning are known as short pruning, half-long pruning, and cane pruning, respectively.

Training, the arrangement of the canes on the trellis, determines shoot arrangement to the extent that it positions the bud or base of the shoot. Its object is to position the leaves for most exposure to light and the fruit for ease of harvest. Selecting well-exposed canes and using the proper severity of pruning are more important than the choice of training system. Actually, the primary objectives in training a young vine are the development of a large healthy root system and straight semipermament trunks. The shaping of the above-ground parts of the vine according to a particular training system is of secondary importance. During the first and second growing seasons, these objectives can best be accomplished by eliminating or reducing the crop and increasing the leaf area. The same treatment rejuvenates very weak vines of any age. As for actual training systems and pruning techniques, check one of the books listed previously in this chapter or with your county agricultural agent.

Sucker and Water Sprout Removal. The removal of suckers and water sprouts from the base and trunk of each vine is referred to as "suckering" or "breaking out." During the first three growing seasons, including the year the vines are planted, all suckers coming up from the ground and water sprouts growing from wood older than one year are "broken out," and the operation completed early in June to insure that shoots growing from one-year-old wood will grow vigorously. Only the shoots growing from the one-year-old wood are left on the vines unless, in the case of three-year-old vines, it is desired to leave a water sprout for a future spur during the following winter's pruning operation.

In the event that some of the buds on the cane of a one- or two-year-old vine do not start, a sucker or water sprout can be left to compensate for each shoot missing on the cane. This can be done if

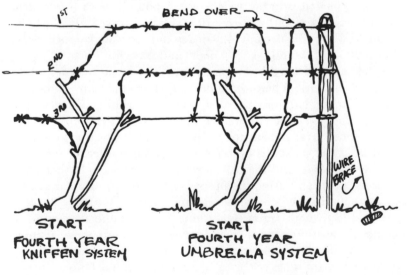

Fig. 34

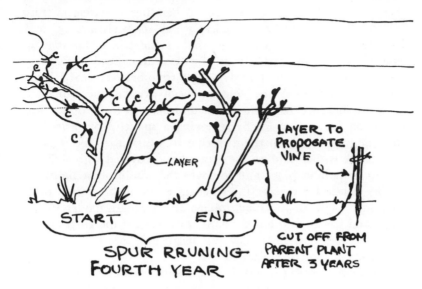

LAYER TO
PROPOGATE
VINE

LAYER

START   END

SPUR RRUNING
FOURTH YEAR

CUT OFF FROM
PARENT PLANT
AFTER 3 YEARS

Fig. 35

a late spring freeze kills shoots on the one-year-old wood and the vine pushes forth suckers after the freeze.

Starting with the fourth growing season, and each season thereafter, only the suckers and water sprouts on the trunk below the head area that are not required for future trunk renewals or spurs need be "broken out."

Winter Protection. It is surprising how well grapes may be grown in the northern section of our country and in Canada if the vines are given proper winter care. First, the following vineyard-management procedures should be followed: pruning should be rather light so as not to induce long, soft growths; nitrogenous fertilizers should be used sparingly; cultivation should be stopped early; and a cover crop should be sown over the vineyard to help mature the wood early. In addition the plants themselves must be protected.

Protecting the plants with an earth cover is far better and cheaper than wrapping them with hay, straw, or other similar material. To cover with earth, the vines must be laid on the ground and thus must be trained for bending. A system of training therefore should be selected in which renewals may be made frequently from the ground so that if the trunks become unpliable a new trunk can be trained which can be readily bent.

The vines should be laid down any time between leaf fall and heavy freezing. After the vine has been pruned, the trunk and arms are loosened from the trellis and bent to the ground. This operation is made easier by removing a spadeful of earth from the side of the vine in the direction in which the vine is to lie. The trunk is then laid on the ground and covered with sufficient soil to keep it in place and to cover the whole plant lightly. It is very important to take the vines up early in the spring. If the covering is left on too long, foliage and vine are tender to sunshine and frost. On the other hand, of course, if the vines are uncovered too early, frost may do harm, but this is unlikely to happen if the earth is thawed.

Disease and Insect Control. The loss of leaves from the young vine shoots before their normal maturity can result in stunted shoot growth and extensive winter-killing of the tops and even entire vines during the following winter. Therefore, it is important to protect the vines from infection of downy and powdery mildew and the depredations of the grape leafhopper and a small, black, jumping beetle called "the redheaded systena." Thus, periodical checks should be made of your young vineyard to make sure that insects and diseases are not "taking over." Your local county agent will help you work out a spray schedule to combat the mildews and insects.

Replacements. Every effort should be made during the first two years after the planting of the vineyard to replace any vines which do not survive. These replacements can be made by filling in with new vines (grade 1-X recommended) in the spring after the first cultivation.

THE VINTAGE

The vintage season was described earlier in Chapter 1, while methods of determining when the grapes are ripe are covered in Chapter 3. Picking shears or curved knives are about the only tools needed to pick grapes and may be purchased at any horti-

Fig. 36: Picking the grapes during the vintage season.

cultural-supply house. The grapes should not be pulled from the vines, but rather clipped with grape shears or knives. Once picked, they should be put in trays and taken to the crushing-pressing area in your winery. The trays may be of any desirable size, but are usually shallow flats holding 20 or 30 pounds of grapes.

A cool, dry, sunny day is the best for picking your grapes. In hot, moist weather, the fruit may start fermentation before it reaches the fermenter. But remember that in not one year out of ten is there a combination of a good season for grapes and perfect weather for picking.

In this chapter we have attempted *only* to highlight the steps involved in growing your own grapes. If you are really interested in viticulture—we believe you should be if you are interested in winemaking—it would be wise to read several of the books listed on page 149.

Appendix A

The Language of Winemaking

In every specialized thing we do, whether it be sewing, fishing, ping pong, or winemaking, there is a specialized language. The winegrowers and wine merchants have theirs, and one who is interested in wine should know their basic vocabulary. The following language of wine also includes wine-tasting terms. You will find such descriptive terms helpful in identifying more exactly the different sensations associated with tasting wines.

Acetic acid. A colorless, pungent substance which is the chief ingredient of vinegar.
Acetification. Turning into acetic acid, vinegar being dilute acetic acid.
Acid. The natural fruit acid of grapes. All premium-quality wines contain it in varying degrees.

Acidity. A word normally used to indicate the quality of tartness or sharpness to the taste; the presence of agreeable fruit acids; an important favorable element in wine quality. Not to be confused with sourness (see *sour*) or with dryness or astringency.

Aftertaste. The olfactory sensation, pleasing in all premium-quality wines, which is produced in the mouth and nasal passages after the wine has been swallowed.

Age. This is often a misleading term. Some wines are at their best when young, even lose their quality after a year or two. Others take years to become mellow, smooth and mature. If the other qualities or characteristics of the wine please, the age is unimportant.

Aged. Wines possessing bottle bouquet.

Aging. The process by which the wine develops smoothness, mellowness, and character.

Alcohol. In winemaking, the result of sweet-grape-juice fermentation. In a naturally fermented wine it usually comprises from 9 to 14 percent of the total volume. In making apéritif and dessert wines, extra alcohol is added in the form of pure grape spirits, bringing the content up to between 17 and 22 percent by volume.

Amelioration. The diluting of the juice slightly with water to lower the total acids.

Apéritif. Usually a wine that has been made by adding a blend of certain herbs and flavoring spices. Vermouth is the most familiar type. Apéritif wines are generally enjoyed before meals to stimulate the appetite.

Appearance. The appearance of a wine is judged upon whether or not the wine seems clear or contains sediment or suspended material of a colloidal or larger-particle size.

Appetizer wine. A wine so called because it is favored for before-meal or cocktail use. The main appetizer wines are sherry and vermouth. They range from extra dry to semisweet.

Aroma. That part of the fragrance of wine which originates from the grapes used.

Aromatized wines. These are apéritif wines made by adding certain herbs and other flavoring elements to wines. They are both dry and sweet.

Astringency. The quality of causing the mouth to pucker. The degree of astringency of a wine depends primarily upon the amount of tannin it has absorbed from the skins and seeds of the grapes. Astringency tends to lessen with bottle age.

Balance. Term used to describe a wine when the many odor and taste substances are present in such quantities that the concerted impression is pleasant. Also a wine possessing the right proportion of sugar and acidity. Such a wine is called *well-balanced*.

Balling. A scale graduation for a hydrometer, or saccharometer, used to read the specific gravity of liquids or their sugar content. Used interchangeably with *Brix*.

Binning. A term used to describe the storing of bottled wines for aging in the bottle.

Blending. The combining, or "marrying," of two or more wine products to obtain a more nearly perfect and uniform-quality wine.

Bloom. The blush on grapes, containing natural yeasts for fermentation.

Body. The consistency, thickness, or substance of a wine, as opposed to the lack of body in a thin, watery wine. A wine full in body such as Burgundy will taste very "winy" and one will prefer to sip it. Wine light in body such as claret may taste watery or thin; it will be easy to swallow.

Bond (in bond). An alcoholic liquor on which the internal revenue tax or duty has not yet been paid is said to be "in bond." It is under government control until the tax or duty has been paid.

Bottle. The usual United States wine bottle holds ⅘ quart or 25.6 fluid ounces; the halves 12.8 fluid ounces. A *magnum* is equivalent to 2 bottles; a *double magnum* or a *jeroboam* to 4 and a *rehoboam* to 6. The usual European wine bottle contains ¾ United States quart or 24 fluid ounces; the halves 12 fluid ounces. (European champagne comes in bottles of 26 fluid ounces and 13 fluid ounces.)

Bottle aging. The standing or aging of a wine or champagne in the bottle.

Bottle fermentation. A secondary fermentation in the bottle which produces effervescence in the wine. This is known as the *true* champagne process.

Bottoms. The same as lees, the deposit in a fermenter or storage container.

Bouquet. That part of the fragrance of wine which originates from the aging; as distinguished from *aroma,* the fragrance of the grape.

Brandy. A spirit distilled from wine.

Brilliant. The quality of a wine free of any visible suspended solids and having a sparkling clarity.

Brix. A scale graduation for a hydrometer, or saccharometer, used in reading the specific gravity of liquids or their sugar content. Used interchangeably with *Balling.*

Brut. A French word usually applied to driest types of champagne.

Bulk process. A method of producing sparkling wine by secondary fermentation in vats instead of bottles, as in the true champagne processes. Also known as *Charmat process.*

Bung. Wooden stopper in a keg or barrel.

Burgundy. Type name used to describe generous, full-bodied dry red dinner wines that are strong in flavor, body, and bouquet, and deep red in color.

Candling: A term given to the process of examining a bottled wine's clarity by holding it before a light.

Capsule. The covering for the opening and neck of a wine bottle used to protect the closure, discourage refilling, and to improve appearance of the bottle. Made of metal foil, plastic, wax, or paper.

Carbonated wines. Sparkling wines produced by injecting carbon dioxide gas into still wines.

Carbon dioxide. A gas given off by grape juice as it ferments. Also the gas generated in champagne by the fermentation-in-the-bottle process.

Carboy. A large glass bottle having a capacity of several gallons.

Cask. Any round, bulging wooden container for wine. Includes puncheons, pipes, butts, tuns, hogsheads, all of which signify various specific measures of capacity in different countries and for various products they may contain. An upright container used for fermenting or storing wine is usually called a *vat* or a *tank*.

Caskiness. A flavor imparted to wine by certain oils which remain in a cask that is not thoroughly clean.

Casse. A white or colored haze that is caused by metallic combinations, such as traces of aluminum, zinc, iron, or copper in the wine. Same as *metal pickup*.

Cellar. A storage place for wine. It need not be below ground.

Cellar treatment. The various processes used in the winery during wine production.

Champagne. Usually a pale gold or straw-colored sparkling dinner wine which has been made naturally effervescent by a second fermentation. The alcoholic content ranges from 11 to 13 percent by volume. There are also a pink champagne and a red champagne (sparkling Burgundy) made in the United States by this process.

Champagne rouge. A red sparkling wine. Usually used to describe a fermented-in-the-bottle sparkling Burgundy.

Character. A term used to define a wine that possesses, to a full degree, the qualities of color, bouquet, and taste associated with a particular type of wine at its best.

Claret. Type name applied to a dry, tart, light- or medium-bodied red dinner wine of ruby red color.

Clarify. To clear up a wine by causing a settlement of the minute particles that make it cloudy or unclear.

Clean. Term used to indicate that a wine is free of any "off" taste. Also applied to a wine that gives the mouth a feeling of refreshing purity —a sense of cleanliness still remains in the mouth and nasal passage after it has been swallowed.

Clear. Wines free of any visible solids but lacking the sparkling clarity of brilliant wines.

Cloudy. Wine which contains varying amounts of suspended particles when disturbed. If cloudiness does not disappear with rest, the wine is most likely undrinkable.

Coarse. Term used to describe the odor and taste in wines of poor balance in which astringency or acidity is excessive. A *harsh* wine is usually similar to a coarse wine but more unpleasant.

Colloidal suspension. A state that exists in liquids when certain semisolid and albuminous particles remain suspended.

Color. Wines obtain their color from the presence of flavonoid compounds that are present in the skins and flesh of the grapes. No coloring substances are permitted in winemaking—all color is from the grapes themselves. This color varies from light straw to deep gold, and all the hues of ruby and garnet. In all premium-quality wines, the color is always as brilliant as gems.

Cooperage. Term used by wineries to designate wine containers, from barrels to large tanks, vats, or casks. The term derives from the occupation of *cooper,* one who makes or repairs barrels.

Cork. Stopper for bottles made from the spongy bark of the cork oak.

Corkscrew. A mechanical device to remove a cork from a wine bottle.

Corky wine. A wine with an unpleasant odor which has been imparted by a defect in the cork. This can happen even with the finest wines and if you get a corky wine your dealer should replace it for you. Term *corkiness* is also used.

Cradle. A receptacle used to hold a bottle of wine at an angle, and from which the wine is poured. Usually made of wicker, wire, or wood.

Cream of tartar. The white crystalline deposit which settles out from wines during cold weather or chilling. A purified form of tartaric acid.

Crust. Deposit of sediment by wine while aging in the bottle; the deposit adheres to the inside of the bottle as a crust.

Cuvée. A blend of new and sometimes aged wines prepared for champagne production.

Decant. To pour wine gently from a bottle in which crust or sediment has deposited, for the purpose of obtaining clear wine for serving. The container into which the wine is thus poured is called a *decanter* or *carafe.*

Delicate. A wine whose subtle, light flavor is fragile and can be destroyed when taken into the mouth with full-flavored food. Some white dinner wines can be classed as delicate.

Demijohn. A wicker-covered wine bottle with a large body and small neck, holding usually from one to five gallons.

Demi-sec. French term for semidry; used to describe sparkling wines.

Dessert wine. The proper name for all sweet or partially sweet still wines containing approximately 17 to 22 percent alcohol by volume, such as port and sherry.

Dinner wine. The proper name for all still wines with not over 14 percent alcohol content by volume. Most dinner wines are dry, but it is wrong to call all dinner wines *dry wines.* That was formerly the practice, but it has been discontinued because many dinner wines, like Sauterne, are actually semisweet or sweet, while some wines of the dessert or appetizer class, like sherry, can be nearly dry. *Dinner wines* is the proper term because most wines of this class are used with meals and the term guides the consumer in selecting the wines for this purpose. The class includes the wines sometimes referred to as *table wines, light wines, dry wines,* or *natural wines.*

Disgorging. The process in which the sediment from the bottle fermentation is removed in the making of champagne.

Dosage. The sweetener added to sparkling wine before the final cork is placed in the bottle.

Doux. French word for sweet; thus applies to a sweet wine, as opposed to *sec* (dry).

Dregs. The lees or sediment precipitated by a wine fermenting in the cask. Loosely applied to the deposit in the bottle.

Dry. The opposite of sweet; i.e., lacking in sweetness. Literally it means lacking in sugar. Fermentation converts the natural sugar of the grape into wine alcohol and carbon dioxide gas. A wine becomes dry when all of the fermentable sugars have been consumed by fermentation.

Enology. The science or the study of winemaking.

Essential oils. Volatile oils that give distinctive odor or flavor to plants, flowers, and fruits. In wine they combine with the alcohol to help determine its bouquet.

Estate bottled. A designation given to a wine that was produced and bottled on the vineyard property where the grapes were grown.

Esters. Wine perfumes formed by the slow chemical interaction of the acids and alcohol in wine.

Extract. An expression of total solids dissolved in a wine.

Extra-dry. A term—employed generally with champagne—indicating the degree of sweetness in the wine. Winemakers' standards vary a great deal in their use of descriptive terms.

False wines. Wines not made from grapes.

Fermentation. The chemical process whereby sugars, by the act of yeast, are broken down into alcohol and carbon dioxide; the changing of the must, or grape juice, into wine.

Fermentation lock. An apparatus which seals a cask or other container of fermenting liquor from the air while permitting the carbon dioxide gas to escape through the water. Same as *water seal,* or *water trap.*

Fermenter. The container in which the grape juice is put to undergo its primary fermentation. Also known as a *vat.*

Fifth. Most popular-size wine bottle in the American market. Contains 25.6 fluid ounces. As the name implies, it is one-fifth of a gallon.

Filtering. The processes of clarifying the wine or removing through filters sediment left by fermentation of the wine.

Fine. To clarify a wine.

Fine wine. A wine of finesse and polish that has developed perfectly.

Fining. The process of settling the sediment from wine during the cellar treatment.

Flat. A wine that is dull and uninteresting, usually because of too-low natural acidity and the poor wine-grape variety used.

Flavored wines. These are grape wines that have had other natural fruit or herb flavors added to them such as May wine. They range from dry to sweet.

Flavorous. The pleasant full flavor taste of wine in the mouth.

Flavors. A term used to describe those complex impressions on the palate created when the wine is rolled over in the mouth.

Flor. A process for sherry by which the aldehydes in sherry flavor are produced by fermentation by flor yeast cells.

Flowers of wine. A white skin which gradually forms on wines exposed to air. This will decompose the wine eventually.

Flowery. A wine with a bouquet that seems to smell of the actual grape blossoms.

Fortified wine. A wine to which grape spirits have been added, thus increasing the natural alcoholic content. Examples: port, sherry. However, this term is seldom used today to describe wines of their type.

Fortify. To raise the alcoholic content of a wine to 18 percent or more by the addition of brandy.

Fruit wines. Wines made from fruits other than grapes. This group includes apple wine, cherry wine, blackberry wine, etc.

Fruity. A term that describes the fresh, tart, generally pleasant fruitlike impression given by well-made young wines. Wines that are not fruity are often called "vinous" or regarded as having a vine taste instead of a fruit taste.

Full. A wine that is pleasingly strong in flavor, taste, or bouquet.

Generic. Wine type names which stand for definite type characteristics are called generic names. Generic names of geographic origin are wine type names originally applied to the wines of specific viticultural districts, but which, when the wines became famous, came gradually through the centuries to designate any wines, wherever grown, which had similar type characteristics. Burgundy, Claret, Port, Rhine wine, Sauterne, Sherry and Champagne are the best-known generic wine type names of geographic origin. Vermouth, on the other hand, is a generic name without geographic significance.

Green. Used to describe wines unbalanced because of excessive acidity. Same as *acidulous* or *unripe*.

Hard. Describes a wine with extreme dryness, with somewhat more acidity than usual. The opposite of mellow or soft.

Harshness. A condition due to lack of age, or to the same causes as "greenness." If the wine is healthy, the condition will often pass with age.

Haut. A term used to describe a wine of the Sauterne type that is sweeter than dry Sauterne.

Heady. Wines of generous or excessive alcoholic content. Same as *strong* or *alcoholic*.

Heavy. A term usually applied to a wine that has an increased alcoholic content, without a corresponding balance of flavor.

Hydrometer. An instrument for measuring the density of liquids. Similar to a *saccharometer*.

Keg. A small cask.

Kniffin. A method commonly used to train grape vines.

Lees. Sediment deposited by wine during fermentation and aging in cooperage.

Light. A term for a pleasing, refreshing wine that is usually on the dry side.

Mature. A term for a wine possessing balanced aged bouquet and ready for bottling.

Mellow. A term for a soft wine that is sometimes slightly on the sweet side.

Moldy. The smell of molds which may appear in wines made from moldy grapes or in wines which have been stored in moldy cooperage.

Must. Unfermented grape pulp.

Musty. A wine that has the odor of damp, decaying wood. This odor does not belong in wine and, should it be present, the wine should be discarded. Same as *mousy wine*.

Natural fermentation. Fermentation carried on under normal conditions and producing an alcoholic strength not greater than that which can be obtained from the sugar in the juice under the conditions of fermentation.

Natural wines. Wines produced by natural fermentation; that is, made naturally, as distinguished from fortified wines.

Nose. A term generally employed by professional wine tasters in describing bouquet; a wine that has a good nose means a wine that has a pleasant bouquet.

Nutty. A term used to describe the desirable odor and nutlike taste of certain appetizer and dessert wines and particularly well-processed sherries. The Spanish call this pungent flavor *rancio.*

Odor. The way the wine smells.

Off-odor. This is an odor which is foreign to the normal odor of a clean, sound wine.

Oxidation. A change in wine, either for good or bad, due to its coming in contact with the air.

Pasteurization. The process of stopping or arresting ferments in wine and other liquids by heating for a period of time to a temperature of between 140° and 180° F.

Perfume. The bouquet of a wine.

Pétillant. Term used to describe wine which has a slight content of carbon dioxide.

Piquant. The French term for a pleasant point of acidity. Generally applied to dry white table wines.

Pomace. The skins and seeds which remain after the pressing of the grapes. Same as *marc.*

Port. A dessert wine which is rich, fruity, full-bodied, and sweet. It is usually deep red in color.

Press. A piece of equipment which forces the juices from the grapes by the application of direct pressure.

Proof. A system of measuring alcoholic strength seldom used for wine. Roughly, one percent by volume is equal to two degrees of proof. For example, a wine with 20 percent alcohol by volume is approximately equal to 40 proof.

Racking. The drawing of wine off its lees from a storage container into a fresh one.

Red dinner wines. Wines of this class are dry, and with their rich, sometimes tart, and even astringent flavors go well with red meats and highly seasoned foods.

Rhine wine. Type name applied to a dry, tart, light-bodied white dinner wine of pale golden color or slightly greenish hue. Similar to a Hock or Riesling wine.

Rich. A term used to describe a full-bodied, flavorous wine. Same as *generous,* or *robust.*

Riddling. The process of working the sediment down into the neck of the bottle during the traditional champagne-making procedure.

Ripe. The term used to describe a wine which has attained full mellowness and perfection and is at its best. When the term *ripe for bot-*

tling is used, it means the wine has improved in storage to the highest point possible, after which aging is usually completed in the bottle.

Ropiness. A fault of wine characterized by viscosity due to lack of astringent matter, chiefly tannic acid.

Rosé. A pink dinner wine, sometimes called a *luncheon* or *all-occasion* wine. Rosé is fruity and ranges from dry to slightly sweet in taste.

Rounded. A wine in which the qualities of body and flavor are united in a harmonious whole. Also *well-rounded*.

Sauterne. A golden-hued, full-bodied white dinner wine which is generally semi-sweet. There are, however, *dry* Sauterne and *haut* Sauterne available.

Scud. A mold which attacks white wines deficient in alcohol. Easily recognized as particles of matter which dart about at the slightest movement of the bottle.

Sec. A French word for *dry*.

Sediment. The solid matter thrown down by a wine in the process of fermentation and aging. It is usually more pronounced in red wines than in white ones. Its presence in a bottle can indicate age, not necessarily spoilage.

Sherry. A wine characterized by its nutty flavor, obtained by aging at a warm temperature through flor yeast fermentation. It ranges in color from pale to dark amber. It is made either dry, medium-dry, or sweet. The sweet type is generally called "Cream sherry."

Siphon. An apparatus, usually consisting of a hose, by which liquids may be transferred to a lower level over an intervening elevation.

Soft. A term used to describe wines of low astringency. This pleasant, ingratiating sensation produced in the mouth is found in well-balanced wines. Same as *smooth*.

Solera. A system of maturing and blending dessert wines.

Sour. A disagreeably acid taste, caused by acetic acid or vinegar. A sour wine is a spoiled wine. *Never* call a dry, astringent, or tart wine "sour."

Sparkling Burgundy. Red Burgundy made to sparkle either by bulk process or by the champagne process.

Sparkling wines. These are wines in which the natural gas (carbon dioxide) accumulated during secondary fermentation is absorbed in the wine while in the bottle (the *true champagne process*) or within a closed vat (see *Bulk process*). This gas rises to the surface, when the wine is uncorked or opened, in the form of tiny effervescent bubbles. Champagne and sparkling Burgundy are examples.

Spicy. A rather agreeable, piquant flavor often encountered in white dinner wines.

Spigot. A faucet usually made of wood which fits into a hole in the end of a cask. It is used to draw off the contents of the cask.

Split. A small bottle (containing either 6.4 or 8 fluid ounces) generally employed for champagne.

Still wines. These are noneffervescent wines in which the natural gas (carbon dioxide) formed during fermentation is allowed to escape. Sauterne, sherry, port, Rhine, Burgundy are examples.

Sweetness. The sensation of sweetness in wines derived mainly from the presence of sugars—glucose and fructose. Glycerol also contributes to the sweet taste, while acidity and astringency counteract the sweet impression.

Tannic acid. An astringent acid necessary to the proper maturing and keeping of wines. Same as *tannin*.

Tart. Possessing agreeable fruit acidity; wines of a pleasing freshness and balance with high acidity usually are described as tart.

Tartaric acid. An acid found in grapes that in its purified form is known as *cream of tartar*.

Taste. True taste sensations are probably limited to the four classes: sour or acid, sweet, bitter, and salt, with the tactile ability to discern viscosity also of importance. In the examination of wines, however, there are a number of other taste sensations—due perhaps to complex interactions of the odor receptors and the taste receptors— which become apparent when the wine is taken into the mouth. For this reason, the taste sensations are listed as acidity, sweetness, body, astringency, and flavors.

Tawny. Red wines when aged for a long time acquire a brownish-red color. It is characteristic of tawny port.

Varietal wine. When a wine is named for the principal grape variety from which it is made, it is said to have a varietal name. Regulations require a varietal-name wine to derive at least 51 percent of its volume, and its characteristic flavor and aroma, from the grape variety whose name is used.

Vermouth. A wine flavored with herbs and other aromatic substances. There are two types—dry (French type) and sweet (Italian type). The dry ranges from water white to pale amber and the sweet is dark amber.

Vinification. The conversion of juice into wine.

Vinosity. The "winy" quality of a wine, especially as regards to flavor, bouquet, and body.

Vintage. The harvesting of grapes, their crushing and fermentation into wine; also the crop of grapes or wine of one season. A *vintage wine* is wine labeled with the year in which all its grapes were gathered and crushed, and the juice therefrom fermented. A *vintage year* is one in which grapes reach full maturity and the wine made from these grapes is of particularly good quality.

Vintner. One who makes wine. The term is used broadly to designate winegrowers, wine blenders and wholesale wine merchants.

Viscidity. A fault of wine which causes it to become viscous or stringy, due to lack of astringent matter, especially tannic acid.

Viticulture. Cultivation of the vine; or the science or study of the production of grapes, or of grapes and wine. Also called *viniculture,* especially when applied to the growing of grapes for wine.

Volatile oil. An oil that readily vaporizes.

White dinner wines. They vary from extremely dry and tart to sweet and full-bodied, with delicate flavor that blends best with white meats, fowl, and seafoods. In color they range from pale straw to deep gold.

Wine. The fermented juice of fresh, ripe grapes, used as a beverage, in cookery, and in religious rites in most parts of the world.

Winegrowing. Because wine is a farm product, produced usually by the grower who cultivates the vineyard and ferments the grapes into wine on the farm, the entire production is referred to as winegrowing, and the producer is called a *winegrower.* Also *winemaker. Never* say "wine manufacturer" or use the word "manufacture" in connection with wine.

Winery. The accurate description of the building or room in which the juice of grapes is fermented into wine.

Woody. The characteristic odor of wet wood is apparent in wines aged for a long period in wooden tanks or casks.

Yeasts. Special strains of yeasts are introduced by modern wineries to start the fermentation of the grape juice. Wild yeasts, commonly found on grapes, will induce a spontaneous fermentation by themselves.

Yeasty. Term used to describe wines containing materials which taste or smell of yeast.

Appendix B

Basic Reference Tables

CONVERSION FACTORS

LENGTH

1 centimeter	0.394	inch
1 inch	2.540	centimeters
1 meter	3.2808	feet
1 foot	0.305	meter
1 meter	1.0936	yards
1 yard	0.9144	meter
1 kilometer	0.62137	mile
1 mile	1.60935	kilometers

CAPACITY

1 milliliter	0.03382 ounce (*U.S. liquid*)
1 ounce (*U.S. liquid*)	29.573 milliliters
1 milliliter	0.2705 dram (*U.S. Apothecaries*)
1 dram (*U.S. Apothecaries*)	3.6967 milliliters
1 liter	1.05671 quarts (*U.S. liquid*)
1 quart (*U.S. liquid*)	0.94633 liter
1 liter	0.26418 gallon (*U.S. liquid*)
1 gallon (*U.S. liquid*)	3.78533 liters

AREA

1 square centimeter	0.1550 square inch
1 square inch	6.452 square centimeters
1 square meter	10.764 square feet
1 square foot	0.09290 square meter
1 square meter	1.1960 square yards
1 square yard	0.8361 square meter
1 square kilometer	0.3861 square mile
1 square mile	2.590 square kilometers
1 acre (*U.S.*)	4840 square yards
1 acre (*U.S.*)	100 hectoacres

VOLUME

1 cubic centimeter	0.0610 cubic inch
1 cubic inch	16.3872 cubic centimeters
1 cubic meter	35.314 cubic feet
1 cubic foot	0.02832 cubic meter
1 cubic meter	1.3079 cubic yards
1 cubic yard	0.7646 cubic meter

MASS

1 gram	15.4324 grains
1 grain	0.0648 gram
1 gram	0.03527 ounce (*Avoirdupois*)
1 ounce (*Avoirdupois*)	28.3495 grams
1 gram	0.03215 ounce (*Troy*)
1 ounce (*Troy*)	31.10348 grams
1 kilogram	2.20462 pounds (*Avoirdupois*)
1 pound (*Avoirdupois*)	0.45359 kilogram

LIQUID MEASURES

Dash	6	drops, about 1/3 teaspoon
Teaspoon	1/8	ounce
Tablespoon	1/2	ounce
Pony	1	ounce
Jigger	1 1/2	ounces
Large jigger	2	ounces
Split, nip, baby	6 1/2	ounces to 8 ounces
Half pint	8	ounces
Tenth (half bottle)	12.8	ounces
Half Bottle (champagne)	13	ounces
Pint	16	ounces
Bottle (wine)	24	and 25.6 ounces
Fifth	25.6	ounces
Bottle (champagne)	26	ounces
Bottle (vermouth) commonly	30	ounces
Quart	32	ounces
Litre	33.8	ounces
Imperial quart	38.4	ounces
Magnum (2 bottles)	52	ounces
Double magnum or jeroboam	104	ounces
Gallon	128	ounces
Tappit-hen	128	ounces; 1 gallon
Rehoboam	156	ounces; 1.22 gallons
Methuselah	208	ounces; 1.625 gallons
Salamanazar	312	ounces; 2.44 gallons
Balthazar	416	ounces; 3.3 gallons
Nebuchadnezzar	520	ounces; 4.07 gallons
Demijohn	627.2	ounces; 4.9 gallons (commonly)
Case—fifths; tenths	307.2	ounces; 2.4 gallons
Case—quarts; pints	384	ounces; 3 gallons

MAKING CHEMICALS AND REAGENTS FOR WINE ANALYSIS

Sodium Hydroxide Normal Over 10 Solution (NaOH N/10)

Weigh up 4.0 grams of (ACS approved or better) NaOH pellets and add enough distilled water to make one liter (1,000 ml).

Should be standardized against N/10 HCl (normal over 10 hydrochloric acid).

Simply pipette 20 ml of your NaOH N/10 solution into a 250-ml Erlenmeyer flask. Fill clean buret with N/10 HCl standard. Add several drops phenolphthalein to NaOH N/10 solution in flask and titrate until pink color disappears. If buret reads more than 20 ml used, your N/10 NaOH is too strong; if less than 20 ml is used to titrate, the N/10 NaOH is too weak. Simply adjust the NaOH solution with water or pellets accordingly.

Iodine Normal Over 40 Solution (I N/40)

Dissolve 3.2 grams of (ACS approved or better) iodine crystals and 6.3 grams of (ACS approved or better) potassium iodide into enough distilled water to total 1 liter (1,000 ml). Mix well and store in refrigerator when not in use. Should be standardized against N/40 sodium thiosulfate solution.

Pipette 20 ml of N/40 I solution into 250-ml Erlenmeyer flask and add several drops of 1% starch solution. Fill clean buret with N/40 sodium thiosulfate solution. Titrate until black color disappears. If more than 20 ml of sodium thiosulfate is needed to neutralize N/40 I, the N/40 I is too strong; correct with more distilled water. If less than 20 ml of sodium thiosulfate is needed the N/40 I is too weak; correct with iodine and sodate crystals in proper proportions.

N/10 I solutions are commonly sold by laboratory supply houses.

To make N/40 I from N/10 I, simply add three times the N/10 I volume in distilled water. Standardize the same way as above.

25% Sulfuric Acid Solution (25% H_2SO_4)

This can oftentimes be purchased at this strength from better hardware stores.

If you purchase concentrated H_2SO_4 solution (95%-98% purity by weight), do not buy fuming H_2SO_4!

First measure out 77 ml of distilled water into a Griffin beaker of about 200-ml capacity or more. Place this beaker into stoppered sink or some other vessel containing cold water. (As you pour concentrated H_2SO_4 into the distilled water an exothermic reaction is taking place; i.e., a reaction that gives off heat. The purpose of cooling the distilled water becomes obvious as a safety measure.)

Now add 23 ml of concentrated H_2SO_4 slowly to the water (*never add water to* H_2SO_4). Allow to sit at least 30 minutes before you pour your 25% H_2SO_4 solution into a storage vessel.

1% Phenolphthalein Solution (1%$C_{20}H_{14}O_4$)

Weigh out ¼ gram of phenolphthalein (powder form) and add to this enough denatured ethyl alcohol to make 25 ml total.

1% Starch Solution (1% $C_6H_{10}O_5$)

Weigh out ¼ gram of soluble starch (powder form). Add this to 25 ml of distilled water and stir. Heat until solution starts to clear nicely (or so that the starch is observed to be dissolving).

Allow to cool (do not refrigerate). Add enough denatured alcohol to bring total volume back to exactly 25 ml.

Yeast Culture Renovation

1. Clean one 250-ml flask.
2. Measure 140 ml of pasteurized grape juice into flask, insert cotton plug.
3. Sterilize flask in pressure cooker with about an inch of water in the bottom, 15 pounds for 15 minutes. Let cool to 5 pounds and release valve.
4. Let flask cool naturally on a towel and inoculate with strain of yeast, taking extreme precaution in sanitary measures. Rotate lip of flask over open flame for 10 to 15 seconds; blow out burning cotton.
5. Allow to ferment 3½ to 4 days.
6. Clean 3 to 5 culture tubes one day before end of item 5 above.
7. Make yeast agar by adding 2¾ grams dextrone triptone agar per 100 ml distilled H_2O and bring to slow boil, being careful not to let boil over.
8. Pour 10 cc agar into each tube and insert cotton plug.
9. Sterilize in pressure cooker as you did flask.
10. While cooling lay on slant to gain large surface of agar for yeast to grow.
11. Drain through cotton plug water that has condensed inside tubes.
12. Transplant yeast from flask to tubes, being extremely cautious in sterile procedures. Burn culture tube lip as you did with flask in step 4.
13. Let ferment on agar for 2 to 4 days, watching growth frequently, and insert in +27° refrigerator.
14. Repeat same procedure every 3 months.

CONVERSION OF DEGREES CENTIGRADE TO DEGREES FAHRENHEIT

Cent.	Fahr.	Cent.	Fahr.
−10	14	21	69·8
− 9	15·8	22	71·6
− 8	17·6	23	73·4
− 7	19·4	24	75·2
− 6	21·2	25	77
− 5	23	26	78·8
− 4	24·8	27	80·6
− 3	26·6	28	82·4
− 2	28·4	29	84·2
− 1	30·2	30	86
0	32	31	87·8
1	33·8	32	89·6
2	35·6	33	91·4
3	37·4	34	93·2
4	39·2	35	95
5	41	36	96·8
6	42·8	37	98·6
7	44·6	38	100·4
8	46·4	39	102·2
9	48·2	40	104
10	50		
11	51·8		
12	53·6		
13	55·4		
14	57·2		
15	59		
16	60·8		
17	62·6		
18	64·4		
19	66·2		
20	68		

CONVERSION OF DEGREES FAHRENHEIT TO DEGREES CENTIGRADE

Fahr.	Cent.	Fahr.	Cent.
42	5·55	74	23·33
43	6·11	75	23·89
44	6·67	76	24·44
45	7·22	77	25
46	7·78	78	25·55
47	8·33	79	26·11
48	8·89	80	26·67
49	9·44	81	27·22
50	10	82	27·78
51	10·55	83	28·33
52	11·11	84	28·89
53	11·67	85	29·44
54	12·22	86	30
55	12·78	87	30·55
56	13·33	88	31·11
57	13·89	89	31·67
58	14·44	90	32·22
59	15	91	32·78
60	15·56	92	33·33
61	16·11	93	33·89
62	16·67	94	34·44
63	17·22	95	35
64	17·78	96	35·55
65	18·33	97	36·11
65	18·33	98	36·67
66	18·89	99	37·22
67	19·44	100	37·78
68	20	101	38·33
69	20·55	102	38·89
70	21·11	103	39·44
71	21·67	104	40
72	22·22		
73	22·78		

CORRECTIONS FOR BRIX AND BALLING HYDROMETERS CALIBRATED AT 68° F.

Temperature of Solution		Observed Percentage of Sugar						
°C.	°F.	0	5	10	15	20	25	30
Below Calibration					Subtract			
15	59.0	0.20	0.22	0.24	0.26	0.28	0.30	0.32
15.56	60.0	0.18	0.20	0.22	0.24	0.26	0.28	0.29
16	60.8	0.17	0.18	0.20	0.22	0.23	0.25	0.26
17	62.6	0.13	0.14	0.15	0.16	0.18	0.19	0.20
18	64.4	0.09	0.10	0.11	0.12	0.13	0.13	0.14
19	66.2	0.05	0.05	0.06	0.06	0.0b	0.07	0.07
Above Calibration					Add			
21	69.8	0.04	0.05	0.06	0.06	0.07	0.07	0.07
22	71.6	0.10	0.10	0.11	0.12	0.13	0.14	0.14
23	73.4	0.16	0.16	0.17	0.17	0.20	0.21	0.21
24	75.2	0.21	0.22	0.23	0.24	0.27	0.28	0.29
25	77.0	0.27	0.28	0.30	0.31	0.34	0.35	0.36
26	78.8	0.33	0.34	0.36	0.37	0.40	0.42	0.44
27	80.6	0.40	0.41	0.42	0.44	0.48	0.52	0.52
28	82.4	0.46	0.47	0.49	0.51	0.56	0.58	0.60
29	84.2	0.54	0.55	0.56	0.59	0.63	0.66	0.68
30	86.0	0.61	0.62	0.63	0.66	0.71	0.73	0.76
35	95.0	0.99	1.01	1.02	6.06	1.13	1.16	1.18

CORRECTIONS FOR HYDROMETERS IN DESSERT WINES AT 20 PERCENT ALCOHOL

Temperature		Observed Balling					
°C.	°F.	0	2.5	5.0	10.0	12.5	15.0
				Subtract			
15	59.0	0.43	0.46	0.49	0.53	0.55	0.57
16	60.8	0.34	0.35	0.39	0.41	0.43	0.44
17	62.6	0.26	0.27	0.27	0.29	0.30	0.31
18	64.4	0.17	0.17	0.19	0.21	0.23	0.25
19	66.2	0.09	0.09	0.09	0.09	0.10	0.11
20	68.0			Add			
21	69.8	0.08	0.08	0.08	0.08	0.09	0.10
22	71.6	0.20	0.17	0.19	0.21	0.23	0.25
23	73.4	0.25	0.27	0.29	0.29	0.30	0.31
24	75.2	0.35	0.37	0.39	0.41	0.43	0.44
25	77.0	0.43	0.45	0.49	0.49	0.51	0.54

SPECIFIC GRAVITY AT 68° F. CORRESPONDING TO
READINGS OF THE BALLING HYDROMETER

Balling	Specific Gravity	Balling	Specific Gravity	Balling	Specific Gravity
Degrees		Degrees		Degrees	
0.00	1.0000	10.0	1.03933	20.0	1.0814
0.50	1.0019	10.5	1.0414	20.5	1.0836
1.00	1.0038	11.0	1.0434	21.0	1.0859
1.50	1.00575	11.5	1.0454	21.5	1.0881
2.00	1.0077	12.0	1.04746	22.0	1.0903
2.50	1.00966	12.5	1.0495	22.5	1.0926
3.00	1.01163	13.0	1.05153	23.0	1.0949
3.50	1.01356	13.5	1.05356	23.5	1.0971
4.00	1.0155	14.0	1.05556	24.0	1.0994
4.50	1.0174	14.5	1.05753	24.5	1.1017
5.00	1.01926	15.0	1.05943	25.0	1.1040
5.50	1.0212	15.5	1.06163	25.5	1.1063
6.00	1.02323	16.0	1.06386	26.0	1.1086
6.50	1.0252	16.5	1.0660	26.5	1.1109
7.00	1.02706	17.0	1.06803	27.0	1.1133
7.50	1.02906	17.5	1.0701	27.5	1.1155
8.00	1.0313	18.0	1.07233	28.0	1.1180
8.50	1.03336	18.5	1.07456	28.5	1.1203
9.00	1.03523	19.0	1.0769	29.0	1.1227
9.50	1.0372	19.5	1.07926	29.5	1.1251
				30.0	1.1274

CORRECTIONS OF ALCOHOL HYDROMETERS CALIBRATED AT 60° F. IN PERCENT BY VOLUME OF ALCOHOL

Observed Alcohol Content	Add at			To or from the Observed — Subtract at																	
Per cent	57 °F.	58 °F.	59 °F.	61 °F.	62 °F.	63 °F.	64 °F.	65 °F.	66 °F.	67 °F.	68 °F.	69 °F.	70 °F.	72 °F.	74 °F.	76 °F.	78 °F.	80 °F.
	Per cent	Per cent	Per cent	Per cent	Per cent	Per cent	Per cent	Per cent	Per cent	Per cent	Per cent	Per cent	Per cent	Per cent	Per cent	Per cent	Per cent	Per cent
1	0.14	0.10	0.05	0.05	0.10	0.16	0.22	0.28	0.34	0.41	0.48	0.55	0.62	0.77	0.93	...	...	...
2	0.14	0.10	0.05	0.05	0.11	0.17	0.23	0.29	0.35	0.42	0.48	0.56	0.63	0.78	0.94	1.10	1.28	1.46
3	0.14	0.10	0.05	0.06	0.12	0.18	0.24	0.30	0.36	0.43	0.50	0.57	0.64	0.80	0.96	1.13	1.31	1.50
4	0.14	0.10	0.05	0.06	0.12	0.19	0.25	0.32	0.38	0.45	0.52	0.59	0.67	0.83	1.00	1.17	1.35	1.54
5	0.15	0.10	0.05	0.07	0.13	0.20	0.26	0.33	0.40	0.47	0.54	0.62	0.70	0.86	1.03	1.21	1.40	1.60
6	0.17	0.11	0.06	0.07	0.14	0.20	0.27	0.34	0.42	0.50	0.57	0.66	0.74	0.90	1.09	1.27	1.46	1.66
7	0.18	0.12	0.06	0.07	0.14	0.21	0.29	0.36	0.44	0.52	0.60	0.68	0.77	0.94	1.13	1.32	1.52	1.73
8	0.19	0.13	0.06	0.08	0.16	0.23	0.31	0.39	0.47	0.55	0.64	0.73	0.81	0.99	1.18	1.38	1.59	1.80
9	0.21	0.14	0.07	0.08	0.16	0.24	0.32	0.41	0.50	0.58	0.67	0.76	0.86	1.04	1.25	1.46	1.67	1.89
10	0.23	0.16	0.08	0.08	0.17	0.25	0.34	0.43	0.52	0.61	0.71	0.80	0.90	1.10	1.32	1.54	1.76	1.99
11	0.25	0.16	0.08	0.09	0.18	0.27	0.37	0.46	0.56	0.65	0.75	0.85	0.96	1.16	1.39	1.61	1.84	2.09
12	0.27	0.18	0.09	0.10	0.20	0.29	0.39	0.49	0.59	0.70	0.80	0.91	1.02	1.23	1.46	1.70	1.94	2.20
13	0.29	0.19	0.10	0.10	0.21	0.31	0.42	0.52	0.63	0.74	0.85	0.97	1.08	1.31	1.55	1.80	2.05	2.31
14	0.32	0.21	0.11	0.11	0.22	0.32	0.44	0.55	0.66	0.78	0.91	1.02	1.14	1.39	1.65	1.91	2.17	2.44
15	0.35	0.23	0.12	0.12	0.24	0.35	0.48	0.60	0.71	0.84	0.97	1.10	1.23	1.50	1.76	2.03	2.30	2.58
16	0.37	0.24	0.12	0.13	0.26	0.38	0.52	0.65	0.77	0.90	1.03	1.17	1.31	1.60	1.88	2.16	2.44	2.72
17	0.40	0.26	0.13	0.14	0.27	0.41	0.54	0.68	0.82	0.96	1.10	1.25	1.40	1.70	1.99	2.28	2.58	2.87
18	0.44	0.29	0.14	0.14	0.29	0.44	0.58	0.73	0.88	1.03	1.18	1.33	1.49	1.80	2.10	2.41	2.72	3.02
19	0.47	0.32	0.16	0.15	0.30	0.46	0.62	0.78	0.94	1.10	1.26	1.42	1.58	1.90	2.22	2.54	2.86	3.17
20	0.51	0.34	0.17	0.16	0.32	0.49	0.66	0.82	0.98	1.15	1.33	1.48	1.65	2.00	2.32	2.65	2.98	3.33
21	0.53	0.35	0.18	0.17	0.34	0.51	0.68	0.85	1.02	1.20	1.38	1.54	1.72	2.06	2.41	2.76	3.10	3.45
22	0.56	0.38	0.19	0.17	0.36	0.53	0.71	0.90	1.07	1.25	1.44	1.61	1.78	2.13	2.48	2.84	3.20	3.56
23	0.58	0.40	0.20	0.18	0.37	0.55	0.74	0.92	1.11	1.30	1.49	1.66	1.84	2.20	2.56	2.93	3.30	3.67
24	0.60	0.40	0.20	0.18	0.38	0.56	0.77	0.96	1.16	1.35	1.54	1.72	1.91	2.27	2.65	3.03	3.40	3.78

PROOF, PERCENT ALCOHOL BY VOLUME AND BY WEIGHT,
AND SPECIFIC GRAVITY AT 60° F.

Proof	Alcohol Per cent by vol.	Alcohol Per cent by wt.	Alcohol Gm. per 100 cc.	Specific Gravity[2]
0.0	0.00	0.00	0.00	1.00000
1.0	0.50	0.40	0.40	0.99923
2.0	1.00	0.79	0.79	0.99849
3.0	1.50	1.19	1.19	0.99775
4.0	2.00	1.59	1.59	0.99701
5.0	2.50	1.99	1.98	0.99629
6.0	3.00	2.39	2.38	0.99557
7.0	3.50	2.80	2.78	0.99487
8.0	4.00	3.20	3.18	0.99417
9.0	4.50	3.60	3.58	0.99349
10.0	5.00	4.00	3.97	0.99281
11.0	5.50	4.40	4.37	0.99215
12.0	6.00	4.80	4.76	0.99149
13.0	6.50	5.21	5.16	0.99085
14.0	7.00	5.61	5.56	0.99021
15.0	7.50	6.02	5.96	0.98959
16.0	8.00	6.42	6.35	0.98897
17.0	8.50	6.83	6.75	0.98837
18.0	9.00	7.23	7.14	0.98777
19.0	9.50	7.64	7.54	0.98719
20.0	10.00	8.04	7.93	0.98660
21.0	10.50	8.45	8.33	0.98603
22.0	11.00	8.86	8.73	0.98546
23.0	11.50	9.27	9.13	0.98491
24.0	12.00	9.67	9.52	0.98435
25.0	12.50	10.08	9.92	0.98381
26.0	13.00	10.49	10.31	0.98326
27.0	13.50	10.90	10.71	0.98273
28.0	14.00	11.31	11.11	0.98219
29.0	14.50	11.72	11.51	0.98167
30.0	15.00	12.13	11.90	0.98114
31.0	15.50	12.54	12.30	0.98063
32.0	16.00	12.95	12.69	0.98011
33.0	16.50	13.37	13.09	0.97960
34.0	17.00	13.78	13.49	0.97909
35.0	17.50	14.19	13.89	0.97859
36.0	18.00	14.60	14.28	0.97808
37.0	18.50	15.02	14.68	0.97758
38.0	19.00	15.43	15.08	0.97708
39.0	19.50	15.84	15.47	0.97658
40.0	20.00	16.26	15.87	0.97608
41.0	20.50	16.67	16.26	0.97558
42.0	21.00	17.09	16.66	0.97507
43.0	21.50	17.51	17.06	0.97457
44.0	22.00	17.92	17.46	0.97406
45.0	22.50	18.34	17.86	0.97355

NOMOGRAPH BETWEEN BALLING OF WINE, EXTRACT, AND
ALCOHOL PERCENT OF DESSERT WINE

To use this chart, place a ruler connecting the two
known values and then read the value of the unknown.

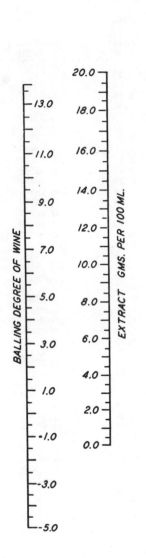

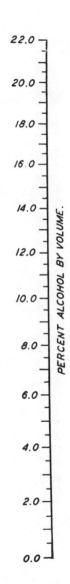

Appendix C

Home Winemaker Supplies

The Winemaker's Shop
Bully Hill Road
Hammondsport, New York 14840

The Compleat Winemaker
614 San Pablo Avenue
Albany, California 94706

Finger Lakes Wine Museum
R.D. 2
Hammondsport, New York 14840

Continental Products, Inc.
Box 26034
Indianapolis, Indiana 46226

Milan Laboratories, Inc.
57 Spring Street
New York, New York 10012

Scott Laboratories, Inc.
860 South Nineteenth Street
Richmond, California 94804

Presque Isle Wine Cellars
5422 Glenwood Park Avenue
Erie, Pennsylvania 16509

Oregon Specialty Company
615 N.E. Sixty-eighth Avenue
Portland, Oregon 97213

Budde & Westermann
116 Glenwood Avenue
Montclair, New Jersey

Semplex of USA
Box 7208
Minneapolis, Minnesota, 55412

F. H. Steinbart Company
526 S.E. Grand Avenue
Portland, Oregon 97214

Wine Record Company
847 Woodstock Road
Olympia Field, Illinois 60461

J. H. Schnier Company
683 Bryant Street
San Francisco, California 94107

Berarducci Brothers Manufacturing Company
Fifth Avenue & Pirl Street
McKeesport, Pennsylvania 15131

Ruttco Manufacturing Company
105-20 Metropolitan Avenue
Forest Hills, New York 11375

Brookside Vineyard Company
Guasti Plaza
Guasti, California 91743

Interstate Products Inc.
Box 1
Pelham, New Hampshire 03076

Boordy Vineyard
Riderwood, Maryland 21139
(Primarily nursery stock)

J. Hill Company
Cuttingsville, Vermont 05738

Vino Corporation
Box 66 NN
East Rochester, New York 14445

Kraus Company
Box 451
Nevada, Missouri 64772

A. R. Zacher Company
Box 1006
Fresno, California 93714

Jim's Home Beverage Supplies
North 2613 Division Street
Spokane, Washington 99207

Stone Hill Wine Company
Hermann, Missouri 65041
(Primarily source of juice)

New York Fruit Testing Association
Geneva, New York 14456
(Nursery stock)

Stribling's Nurseries
Merced, California 95340
(Nursery stock)

Johnston Vineyards
4320 North Barnes
Oklahoma City, Oklahoma 73112
(Nursery stock)

Index

70 71 72 73 10 9 8 7 6 5 4